CHOICES

ELEMENTARY STUDENTS' BOOK

MICHAEL HARRIS • ANNA SIKORZYŃSKA

CONTENTS

Lesson/page	Language	Skills
3 DOWNTOWN		
Topic Talk (p. 31)	**Vocabulary network:** Going out **Pronunciation:** Silent *r*	**Listening:** Favourite places **Speaking:** Talking about your town/city
7 Clubs (pp. 32-33)	**Grammar:** Comparatives **Grammar Alive:** Comparing places	**Reading:** Forum about clubs for teenagers **Listening:** Dialogue about two cafés
8 Free Fun (pp. 34-35)	**Word Builder:** Verbs and prepositions **Sentence Builder:** Time prepositions: *in/on/at*	**Reading:** Tourist information website (Gap fill) **Listening:** Recorded information for London attractions (Gap fill)
9 Skaters (p. 36)	**Grammar:** Superlatives **Grammar Alive:** Talking about cities	**Reading:** Article about skateboarding on the Southbank **Listening:** The UK's best city
Speaking Workshop 3 (p. 37)	**Talk Builder:** Asking for information **Pronunciation:** Intonation (questions)	**DVD Choice:** Asking for information **Speaking:** Information about concerts (Role-play)
Writing Workshop 2 (p. 38)	**Text Builder:** Informal expressions **Sentence Builder:** *and/but*	**Reading/Writing:** Short notes and replies
4 MEMORIES		
Topic Talk (p. 39)	**Vocabulary network:** Birthday memories **Pronunciation:** Dates	**Listening:** Three descriptions of birthdays **Speaking:** Talking about your birthday memories
10 School Days (pp. 40-41)	**Grammar:** Past Simple **Grammar Alive:** Excuses	**Reading:** A school memory **Listening:** Excuses **Speaking:** Making excuses (Role-play)
11 Meeting People (pp. 42-43)	**Word Builder:** Adverbs **Sentence Builder:** Time linkers	**Reading:** Article about family memories (T/F) **Writing:** Describing a memory
12 Witnesses (p. 44)	**Grammar:** Past Simple questions **Grammar Alive:** Questioning	**Reading:** Interview about a burglar
Speaking Workshop 4 (p. 45)	**Talk Builder:** Talking about memories **Pronunciation:** Intonation (sentences)	**DVD Choice:** Talking about memories **Speaking:** Talking about a memory
Language Review (p. 46)	**Revision:** (Gap fill)	
5 FITNESS		
Topic Talk (p. 47)	**Vocabulary network:** Exercise **Pronunciation:** Silent letters	**Listening:** Dialogue about exercise **Speaking:** Talking about your exercise
13 Super Athletes (pp. 48-49)	**Grammar:** Present Continuous **Grammar Alive:** Describing a scene	**Reading/Listening:** Dialogue about an unusual athlete
14 Get Fit (pp. 50-51)	**Sentence Builder:** *too/not enough* **Word Builder:** Multi-part verbs (2)	**Reading:** Adverts for fitness activities (Matching) **Listening:** Dialogues about fitness (Matching, T/F)
15 A Fitness Freak (p. 52)	**Grammar:** Present Continuous – arrangements **Grammar Alive:** Talking about arrangements	**Reading/Listening:** Dialogue about a fitness freak
Speaking Workshop 5 (p. 53)	**Talk Builder:** Requests and replies **Pronunciation:** Intonation (requests)	**DVD Choice:** Requests and replies **Speaking:** Requests (Role-play)
Writing Workshop 3 (p. 54)	**Text Builder:** Accepting and refusing invitations **Sentence Builder:** Linkers *because* and *so*	**Reading/Writing:** Writing an invitation
Culture Choice 2 (pp. 98-99)	**Story:** Extract from *My family and Other Animals* **Project:** Biography of a famous person	

CONTENTS

A ME

1 Vocabulary Look at the vocabulary box below. Write down the countries and numbers.

AUS – Australia
18 – eighteen

Countries: AUS, BG, GB, PL, H, E, I
Numbers: 18, 33, 55, 15, 8, 22, 49

Countries
Argentina, Australia, Brazil, Britain, Bulgaria, Czech Republic, Hungary, Italy, Poland, Romania, Russia, Spain, Turkey, Ukraine, the USA

Numbers
oh/zero, one, two, three, four, five, six, seven, eight, nine, ten, eleven, twelve, thirteen, fourteen, fifteen, sixteen, seventeen, eighteen, nineteen, twenty, twenty-one, twenty-two, thirty, thirty-three, forty, forty-one, fifty, fifty-five

---

2 `1.2` **Listen to a conversation. Who are the people (a–b) in the photo below?**

1 a language student
2 a teacher
3 the school secretary

3 `1.2` **Listen again to the conversation. Complete the information.**

My name's Cristina Conti, I'm from ¹ *Italy* .
I'm ²_____ years old.
My address is ³_____ San Vitale Street, Bologna.
My phone number is ⁴39-351-_____ .

4 `1.3` **Pronunciation** Listen and repeat the words from the vocabulary box.

1 *fifteen*

LANGUAGE CHOICE 1: VOCABULARY PRACTICE

5 Read the dialogue. Where are the people from?

1 Barbara   *Britain*
2 Cristina   4 Mario
3 Tom   5 Erika

A: Hello, … er, are you a teacher?
B: Hello, I'm Barbara. I'm not a teacher – I'm the school secretary.
A: Oh, … hi.
B: What's your name?
A: My name's Cristina Conti.
B: Where are you from?
A: I'm from Italy.
B: How old are you?
A: I'm sixteen years old.
B: And what's your address?
A: It's 21 San Vitale Street, Bologna, Italy.
B: What's your telephone number?
A: My phone number is 39-351-267-7172.
B: Okay, thanks, Cristina.
A: Who is my teacher?
B: Your teacher is Mr Roberts. His name is Tom.
A: Is he from Britain?
B: No, he isn't. He's from Australia. He's really nice.
A: Good!
B: Now come and meet two students – they are in your class. Their names are Mario and Erika. Mario's from Argentina and Erika's from Hungary.

Cristina Conti
21 San Vitale Street
Bologna
Italy

to be and *I/my, you/your* etc.

6 Read the dialogue in Exercise 5 again. Complete the table below with *'m not , isn't , 'm, 's* (x 2).

Affirmative		
I	[1] *'m* **(am)**	sixteen years old.
You/We/They	**'re (are)**	from Argentina and Hungary.
He/She/It	[2] _____ **(is)**	from Australia.
Negative		
I	[3] _____ **(am not)**	a teacher.
You/We/They	**aren't (are not)**	from Italy.
He/She/It	**isn't (is not)**	from Britain.

Yes/No questions			Short answers	
Am	I	in your class?	Yes, I **am**.	No, I **'m not**.
Are	you/we/they	in my class?	Yes, you/we/they **are**.	No, you **aren't**.
Is	he/she/it	from Britain?	Yes, he/she/it **is**.	No, he/she/it [4] ___ **(is not)**.

Wh- questions
What**'s** your name?
Where **are** you from?
How old **are** you?
Who [5] _____ my teacher?

7 **1.4** Pronunciation Listen and repeat the contractions.

➤ LANGUAGE CHOICE 2 AND 3

8 Complete the sentences from the dialogue in Exercise 5 with the words below.

> their   you   his   ~~my~~   it

Subject pronouns	Possessive adjectives
I'm from Italy.	[1] *My* name's Cristina.
How old are [2] _____ ?	What's **your** address?
He's from Australia.	[3] _____ name is Tom.
She's from Hungary.	**Her** name is Erika.
[4] _____ 's 21 San Vitale Street.	**Its** name is San Vitale.
We're in your class.	Who's **our** teacher?
You are in his class.	**Your** teacher is Tom.
They are in your class.	[5] _____ names are Mario and Erika.

➤ LANGUAGE CHOICE 4

9 Use the tables in Exercises 6 and 8 to complete the dialogues.

A: Hi. What's [1] *your* name?
B: [2] _____ name's Cristina. Are you Tom?
A: No, [3] _____ not. I'm Sam.
A: Where [4] _____ you from? Are you from Australia?
B: No, I'm not. Liz and I are from Britain. [5] _____ 're from London.
A: What are [6] _____ names?
B: Her name's Erika and [7] _____ name's Adam.
A: Where are [8] _____ from?
B: They're from Hungary.

10 Write notes about your personal information.

Name: Luis From: Madrid Age: 15
Phone number: 3461-998-7777
Address: 31 Bravo Murillo Street …

11 Work in pairs. Use the cues below to ask and answer questions.

1 what / name?
A: *What's your name?*
B: *My name's Ivan.*
2 how old?
3 what / telephone number?
4 what / address?

Classroom Language

12 **1.5** Read and listen to the alphabet. Then listen and write down the words.

1 *Britain*

Aa/Bb/Cc/Dd/Ee/Ff/Gg/Hh/Ii/Jj/Kk/Ll/Mm/Nn/Oo/Pp/Qq/Rr/Ss/Tt/Uu/Vv/Ww/Xx/Yy/Zz

13 **1.6** Pronunciation Listen and repeat the dialogues in the box below.

14 Work in pairs. Ask questions about the spelling of names and words from this lesson.

> *Asking about spelling*
>
> A: **Can you spell** your name, please?
> B: T-H-O-M-A-S
> A: **Can you spell** address?
> B: A-D-D-R-E-S-S

B MY CLASS

❶ Vocabulary Look at the vocabulary box below. Match the symbols (1-7) with the instructions (a-g).

1 *b*

Instructions

a **Work** in pairs/groups.
b **Open** your book on page five. **Read** the text. **Use** a dictionary.
c **Listen to** the dialogue.
d **Look at** the photos. **Watch** the DVD.
e **Match** the photos with the sentences.
f **Write** five sentences in your notebook. **Complete** the table. **Do** Exercise 5.
g **Ask** and **answer** questions. **Tell** your partner about your interests. **Speak** English.

❷ Read the lesson instructions and complete them with verbs from the vocabulary box.

'Good morning. Please ¹ *open* your books on page thirty-two. Okay, now ² _____ at the photos of three sports stars. Who is your favourite star? Now ³ _____ the text and ⁴ _____ the photos with the sentences. Don't ⁵ _____ a dictionary. Good. Now, ⁶ _____ to the dialogue and ⁷ _____ the questions about football. Now ⁸ _____ in pairs. Ask and answer questions about your favourite football club. Don't ⁹ _____ Spanish!'

❸ [1.7] Listen and check your answers.

Imperatives

❹ [1.8] Pronunciation Listen and repeat the imperatives.

Affirmative	Negative
Use a dictionary.	**Don't use** a dictionary.
Look at your books.	**Don't look at** your books.
Speak English.	**Don't speak** Spanish.

➤ LANGUAGE CHOICE 5

❺ Use the cues to write affirmative and negative sentences.

1 your mobile phone in class / your mobile at home

   Don't use your mobile phone in class. Use your mobile phone at home.

2 your language in English class / English
3 a dictionary in class / a dictionary in exams
4 sentences in the coursebook / in your notebook
5 to your teacher in class / your MP3 player in class
6 your homework at home / your homework in the lesson

❻ Work in groups. One student look at page 116 and read the instructions. The last student to do something is out of the game.

Classroom Language

❼ [1.9] Pronunciation Listen and repeat the sentences below.

Asking for repetition
A: I don't understand. **Can you repeat that, please?**
B: Sorry, **can you** play the CD **again, please?**

❽ Work in pairs. Take turns to be a teacher and a student. Give your partner instructions. Ask him/her to repeat when you can't understand or hear.

A: *Open your book on page fifteen.*
B: *Sorry, can you repeat that, please?*

C MY ABILITIES

can/can't

3 Complete the sentences from the dialogue with *can* or *can't* (*cannot*).

Affirmative		
I/You/He/ She/It/We/ You/They	1 _can_	swim and ski.
Negative		
I/You/He/ She/It/We/ You/They	2 _____	play an instrument.
Questions		
3 _____	I/you/he/ she/it/we/ you/they	play tennis?
Short answers		
Yes, I/you/he/she/it/we/ you/they 4_____ .		No, I/you/he/she/it/we/you/ they 5_____ .

1 **Vocabulary** Match the topics (1–4) with the abilities (a–d).

1 art/creativity *c*   3 technology
2 sport   4 languages

Abilities

a count to 100 in French, say the alphabet in English, speak Spanish, spell my name in German, tell the time in Italian

b play basketball/football/tennis, ride a bicycle/ horse, ski, swim 100 metres

c dance, draw, paint, play an instrument (the piano/violin/guitar), sing, write stories

d download music, find information on the internet, upload photos

4 **1.11** **Pronunciation** Listen and repeat the sentences.

 LANGUAGE CHOICE 6

5 Correct these sentences about Tracy and Jack.

1 Tracy can't play tennis.
  Tracy can play tennis.
2 She can play the piano.   5 He can ski.
3 She can't sing.   6 He can't play football.
4 Jack can't speak languages.

2 **1.10** Read and listen to a classroom dialogue. List the abilities of Tracy and Jack.

Tracy – swim/ski

Teacher: So, Tracy, what sports can you do?
Tracy: Well, I can swim and ski.
Teacher: Can you play tennis?
Tracy: Yes, I can.
Teacher: Can you play a musical instrument?
Tracy: No, I can't play an instrument. But I can sing and dance.
Teacher: And computers? What things can you do?
Tracy: I can upload photos and download music.
Teacher: Tell the class about your partner, Jack.
Tracy: He can speak French. And he can count to 100 in Russian.
Teacher: Can he ski?
Tracy: No, he can't. But he can ride a bicycle and play football.

6 Work in pairs. Use the vocabulary in Exercise 1 to ask and answer questions about your abilities.

A: *Can you count to 100 in English?*
B: *Yes, I can.*

Classroom Language

7 **1.12** **Pronunciation** Listen and repeat the dialogues below.

8 Work in pairs. Test your partner's vocabulary from Lessons A to C.

Asking for meaning

A: **What's** *notebook* **in** French?
B: *Cahier.*
A: **What's** *caballo* **in** English?
B: *Horse.*

D MY STUFF

1 Vocabulary **Look at the box below. Find the words for the objects above (photos a-d). What are *your* favourite things?**

Objects
bag, book, CD, computer, earrings, football, guitar, mobile phone, MP3 player, painting, photo, poster, scarf, shoes, tennis racquet, T-shirt

Adjectives
beautiful, big/small, cheap/expensive, great, old/new, special

Colours
black, blue, brown, green, grey, orange, pink, purple, red, white, yellow

2 1.13 **Read and listen to Vanessa's description. Find four differences with the photos (a-d).**

1 *Her scarf is grey and pink.*

This is my favourite thing. It's not expensive but this scarf is special for me. It's a birthday present from my boyfriend, Tom. Green and grey are my favourite colours. That's a photo of my grandma and me. It is from my birthday. These are my earrings. I really like earrings! These red earrings here are from our holiday in Greece. They're beautiful! Those are my posters over there. Those posters are of my favourite singers – Beyoncé and Rihanna.

this, that, these, those

3 1.14 **Pronunciation Look at the sentences from the description. Listen and repeat the sentences.**

Singular
This is my favourite thing. ***This*** scarf is special.
That's a photo of my grandma. ***That*** photo is from my birthday.

Plural
These are my earrings. ***These*** red earrings here are from our holiday.
Those are my posters over there. ***Those*** posters are of my favourite singers.

→ LANGUAGE CHOICE 7

4 **Complete the sentences with *this, that, these* or *those*.**

1 Come here. Look at ___this___ new mobile phone. It's great!
2 What are _____ things over there? Are they old CDs?
3 Are _____ your books? Or are _____ your books over there?
4 Look over there. _____ is my favourite photo.
5 Look at _____ here. It's my new phone.

5 **Work in pairs. Ask and answer questions about things in the classroom.**

A: *Is this your coursebook?*
B: *No, it isn't. That's my coursebook over there.*

coursebook   notebook   pen   pencil
dictionary   activity book   bag

Possessive 's

6 🔊1.15 Read and listen to Vanessa's description of the things in her house. What are her family's interests?

Her dad – painting

These paintings are my dad's – he can paint fantastic pictures. These CDs are my mum's – she's very musical. And those are my parents' books over there. That guitar is Chris's – he's my brother and he can play the piano and the guitar. Those are Tess's shoes – she's my sister and she's twenty years old.

7 Look at the table and add words in blue from the description in Exercise 6.

Apostrophe for possession	
Singular nouns:	Tom's, Vanessa's, *dad's*, _____
Singular nouns with s endings:	Charles's, Frances's, _____ , _____
Plural nouns:	my partners', our teachers', _____

8 🔊1.16 **Pronunciation** Listen and repeat the words.

➥ LANGUAGE CHOICE 8

9 Underline the correct word.

1 *Tom/Tom's* is my friend. I like *Tom/Tom's* new mobile but *Tom/Tom's* favourite thing is his computer. It's great!
2 This is *Frances/Frances's* dictionary. *Frances/Frances's* can speak three languages. *Frances/Frances's* mum is from Spain and her dad is from the USA.
3 My *friends/friends'* can ski, swim and play tennis. My *friends/friends'* favourite sport is tennis. Here are two photos of my *friends/friends'*.

Possessive pronouns

10 🔊1.17 Read and listen to Vanessa's description. List the people's objects.

Vanessa – tennis racquet

• Vanessa   • Chris
• her grandparents   • her mum

Okay, those things over there are my grandparents' – that old piano's theirs. These things are ours. This tennis racquet is mine and that racquet is Chris's. And that football's his. This is my mum's old computer and those CDs are hers.

11 Complete the sentences with words in blue from Exercise 10.

Possessive adjectives	Possessive pronouns
This is **my** tennis racquet.	This tennis racquet is ¹ *mine* .
That is **your** book.	That book is **yours**.
That is **his** football.	That football's ² _____ .
Those are **her** tennis shoes.	Those tennis shoes are ³ _____ .
These are **our** things.	These things are ⁴ _____ .
That is **their** piano.	That piano is ⁵ _____ .

➥ LANGUAGE CHOICE 9

12 Complete the sentences with possessive adjectives and pronouns.

1 Dave is good with computers. ___*His*___ computer is expensive.
2 We are from London. _____ football team is Arsenal.
3 This book is _____ . It is a present from my mum.
4 Sue is musical and this violin is _____ .
5 Is this pen _____ ? Can I use it, please?
6 Tom is good at tennis. This racquet is _____ .

Classroom Language

13 🔊1.18 **Pronunciation** Listen and repeat the dialogues below.

> *Asking to use things*
>
> A: **Can I use** your pencil, please?
> B: **Sorry**. I need it.
> C: **Of course** you can. Here you are.

14 Work in pairs. Ask and answer questions about the objects in Exercise 5.

A: *Is this dictionary yours?*
B: *Yes, it's mine.*
A: *Can I use it, please?*
B: *Sorry. I need it.*

11

E MY FAMILY

1 Vocabulary **Look at the vocabulary box below and the photo of Jamie's family. Who are the people?**

Sarah is Jamie's mum.

Family
parents, father (dad), mother (mum)
brother, cousin, daughter, husband,
sister, son, wife
grandparents, grandfather
(granddad), grandmother (grandma),
granddaughter, grandson

Appearance
blue, brown, green, grey **eyes**
black, blond, dark, fair, grey, red **hair**
long, short **hair**
attractive, nice smile, overweight,
short, slim, tall

Adjectives
friendly, happy, hard-working,
interesting, sociable, sporty

2 1.19 **Read and listen to an interview with Jamie. Write notes about the appearance of the people in Jamie's family (his grandma, Claire, Ruby and his granddad).**

Jamie's granddad - grey hair

Kathy: So what are your parents' names, Jamie?
Jamie: Sarah and Eric.
Kathy: Have you got brothers or sisters?
Jamie: Yes, I've got three sisters. But I haven't got a brother.
Kathy: Are your sisters at this school?
Jamie: Claire and Emma are at this school. Claire's seventeen and Emma is fifteen. Ruby's at primary school. She's five and she's got blond hair.
Kathy: And Claire - has she got blond hair?
Jamie: No, she hasn't. Claire's different from Emma, Ruby and me. We've got blond hair and blue eyes. Claire's tall and she's got brown eyes and long, brown hair. She's very sporty. Look, I've got a family photo.
Kathy: Ah, is this your grandma? She's got a nice smile.
Jamie: Yes, she's very friendly.
Kathy: And your granddad, he hasn't got blond hair.
Jamie: No, he's got grey hair.

have/has got

3 Complete the sentences with words in blue from the dialogue.

Affirmative		
I/You/We/They	¹ _'ve_ **got** (have got)	three sisters.
He/She/It	² _____ **got** (has got)	brown eyes.
Negative		
I/You/We/They	³ _____ **got** (have not got)	a brother.
He/She/It	**hasn't got** (has not got)	blond hair.

Questions				Short answers
⁴ _____	I/you/we/ they	**got**	brothers or sisters?	Yes, I/you/we/they **have**. No, I/you/we/they **haven't**.
⁵ _____	he/she/it	**got**	blond hair?	Yes, he/she/it **has**. No, he/she/it ⁶ _____ .

4 〔1.20〕 **Pronunciation** Listen and repeat the contractions.

↘ LANGUAGE CHOICE 10

5 Correct the sentences about Jamie's family.

1 Ruby has got two brothers.

Ruby has got two brothers. No, she hasn't.
Ruby has got one brother.

2 Eric and Sarah have got two daughters.
3 Dave has got one granddaughter.
4 Ruby's brother has got brown hair.
5 Claire and Eric have got grey hair.
6 Eric and Jamie have got long hair.

6 Complete the dialogue.

Jason: ¹ _Have_ you got brothers or sisters?
Chloe: Yes, I ² _____ got one brother, Tim. But I ³ _____ got a sister. Tim is eighteen years old and he's tall and slim.
Jason: ⁴ _____ your brother got blond hair?
Chloe: No, we're different – Tim ⁵ _____ got blond hair. He ⁶ _____ got long brown hair.
Jason: Have your mum and dad ⁷ _____ blond hair?
Chloe: Yes, they ⁸ _____ . But my dad's got very short hair and my mum and I have got long hair.

7 Write notes about your family and their appearance.

two sisters – Anna and Magda
Anna – brown hair/blue eyes

8 Work in pairs. Use your notes to ask and answer questions about your families.

A: *Have you got a brother?*
B: *Yes, I have. He's twenty-one. He's got ...*

Classroom Language

9 Order the days of the week.

Days
Wednesday, Sunday, Friday, Monday, Thursday, Saturday, Tuesday

10 〔1.21〕 Listen and repeat the dialogue below.

Asking about homework
Student: Have we got homework?
Teacher: Yes, you have.
Student: What is it?
Teacher: Do Exercise 6 on page twenty-one.
Student: When's it for?
Teacher: For Friday.

11 Work in pairs. Ask and answer questions about homework.

13

F MY LESSONS

1 Vocabulary **Match the pictures (a-d) with four school subjects in the vocabulary box below.**

a *ICT*

Subjects
English, French, geography, history, information and computer technology (ICT), maths, physical education (PE), science, Spanish

2 [1.22] **Listen to three lesson extracts. What subjects are they from?**

3 [1.23] Pronunciation **Look at the vocabulary box. Listen and repeat the times.**

4 **Look at the times in the box. Write down the times of your lessons. What lessons are your favourites?**

Monday: Half past eight - science.
Twenty-five to ten - maths.
Quarter past eleven - English. English is my favourite!

Times
twenty to ten, quarter to eleven, five to twelve, twelve o'clock, five past one, quarter past three, half past four

➥ LANGUAGE CHOICE 11: VOCABULARY PRACTICE

Object pronouns

5 [1.24] Pronunciation **Listen and repeat the pronouns. What are they in your language?**

Subject pronouns	Object pronouns
I	Tell **me** about it.
you	Can I ask **you** a question?
he	Ask **him**.
she	Ask **her**.
it	Ask about **it**.
you	Can I ask **you** a question?
we	Tell **us**.
they	Look at **them**.

➥ LANGUAGE CHOICE 12

6 **Complete the sentences with object pronouns.**

1 Read the text and answer questions about __it__ .
2 Look at the photos and match _____ with the sentences.
3 Work with Tom. Ask _____ questions.
4 We don't understand. Please, help _____ .
5 Ana, tell the class about your abilities. Sam, listen to _____ .
6 Sorry, Carol. I can't tell _____ the answer.

Classroom Language

7 [1.25] Pronunciation **Listen and repeat the questions and replies.**

Asking for permission

Student: **Can** I go to the toilet, please?
Teacher: **Of course you can**.
Student: **Can** I close the window, please?
Teacher: **Sorry, you can't**.

8 **Work in pairs. Take turns to ask permission for these things.**

• Open/close the window/door. • Go to the toilet.
• Use a dictionary/my computer/my mobile phone.
• Speak in my language.

1 LIFESTYLES

Objectives: Listen, read and **talk about** interests and lifestyles; **meet** people, **ask** how they are and **say** goodbye; **write** an email; **learn about** the Present Simple.

TOPIC TALK

1 Look at the photos (a–c). Find the people's interests and activities in the network.

2 [1.26] [1.27] Listen to the people in the photos (a–c). Check your guesses from Exercise 1. Add two interests for each person.

Kate: dancing, cinema

3 [1.28] [1.29] Listen again to the first person. Complete the information in the network.

a Kate

b Ben

c Mandy

My interests

I like ¹ *dancing* and ² _____ .
In the ³*morning/afternoon/evening*,
I ⁴ _____ .
On Saturday, I ⁵ _____ .
On Sunday, I ⁶ _____ .

Interests
computer games, computers, dancing, fashion, films, football, music, photography, reading, shopping, sport, swimming, tennis

Free time activities
buy things/**chat** with my friends online, **do** sport, **go** shopping/swimming/running, **go out** with my friends, **go to** the cinema/discos/parties, **listen to** music, **play** computer games/football/tennis/basketball, **relax** at home, **use** the internet, **watch** TV/films

4 [1.30] **Pronunciation** Listen and write the sentences. <u>Underline</u> the stressed words.

In the <u>evening</u>, I <u>use</u> the <u>internet</u>.

↘ LANGUAGE CHOICE 13:
VOCABULARY PRACTICE

5 Work in groups. Use the network to talk about *your* interests.

GRAMMAR
THE SUPER-RICH

Warm Up

1 Look at the photos (a–b). Use the adjectives below to describe the people.

- rich
- interesting
- happy
- busy
- friendly
- hard-working

2 Read about two super-rich teenagers. Which lifestyle is interesting for you?

(1.31)

London is the world capital of the super-rich. A lot of billionaires live there. Meet two of London's richest teenagers.

Robert (19) is a history student at University College London. He lives in a small house with four good friends. They like shopping in the local market and they cook their dinners together. Robert always goes to college on his bike. He doesn't use a car. He says, 'My family is rich but my teachers and friends don't know about it. My day starts at 6.30 in the morning. I cycle to college and to work. I work in a bookshop on Fridays and Saturdays and I often play football in the park. My life is ve ordinary.'

Lindsay (18) never starts her day before 9 a.m. In the morning, she goes swimming in her private swimming pool and then she usually goes shopping in her Range Rover. She doesn't do housework and she doesn't like studying. In the afternoon, she sometimes plays golf and in the evening, she goes out with her friends. She says, 'My friends come from rich families, too. We don't study or work. We love parties and often go to discos. I don't want to work. My parents work hard and they're always tire

Present Simple

3 Complete the sentences from the text with *go/goes* (affirmative) or *don't/doesn't* (negative). Then complete the rules.

Affirmative	Negative
I **play** football on Fridays.	I **don't want** to work hard.
You **know** rich teenagers.	You **don't go** to school.
He **lives** in a small house.	He ³_____ use a car.
She ¹ _goes_ shopping.	She **doesn't like** studying.
My day **starts** at 6.30 in the morning.	Her day **doesn't start** early.
We ²_____ to discos.	We ⁴_____ study
You **have** fun.	You **don't work**.
They **come** from rich families.	They **don't know** about it.

Affirmative
- The verb has _____ at the end with *he/she/it*.

Negative
- We use _____ with *he/she/it*.
- We use _____ with *I/you/we/they*.

4 Read the rule. Match the sentences (a–b) with the uses (1–2). Find more examples of each use in the text.

a *We **love** parties.*
b *I **work** in a bookshop on Fridays and Saturdays.*

We use the Present Simple to talk about:

1 things that happen regularly.
2 things that are true in general.

Practice

5 Complete the sentences with the verbs in the Present Simple.

1 Over seventy billionaires _live_ (live) in New York.
2 Children of the super-rich _____ (go) to private schools.
3 Rich people often _____ (not like) expensive clothes.
4 Bill Gates _____ (eat) hamburgers.
5 A rich person _____ (not understand) a poor person's problems.

LANGUAGE CHOICE 14

6 Complete the text with the verbs in the correct form of the Present Simple.

Francesca ¹ _comes_ (come) from a family of billionaires but she ² _____ (not talk) about it very often. Her parents ³ _____ (live) in a big house in London. Her father ⁴ _____ (work) in his bank and her mother ⁵ _____ (not work). Francesca ⁶ _____ (go) to a private school. On Saturdays, she often ⁷ _____ (play) tennis. On Sundays, Francesca and her family ⁸ _____ (go out) to have dinner in an expensive restaurant. Francesca and her brothers ⁹ _____ (not like) the restaurant, they ¹⁰ _____ (like) home-cooked dinners.

7 Read the sentences in the Sentence Builder. Put *always* and *never* in the correct places. Then read sentences 1 and 2 and underline the correct word in the rules below.

Sentence Builder Adverbs of frequency

100% Robert _____ goes to college on his bike.
80% After breakfast, Lindsay **usually** goes shopping.
60% Robert **often** plays football in the park.
30% In the afternoon, Lindsay **sometimes** plays golf.
0% Lindsay _____ starts her day before 9 a.m.

---

1 We **often** go to discos.
2 They're **always** tired.

- The adverb of frequency goes *before/after* the verb be.
- The adverb of frequency goes *before/after* other verbs.

LANGUAGE CHOICE 15

8 Use the adverbs below and the sentences (1-6) to write true sentences about you. Remember the correct position of the adverbs.

always usually often sometimes never

1 I do homework at night.
   I usually do my homework at night.
2 I buy things online.
3 I watch horror films.
4 I play football on Sundays.
5 I listen to music in the morning.
6 I'm happy on Monday mornings.

Grammar Alive
Talking about habits

9 [1.32] Listen to the conversation between Josh and Katie and complete the sentences with the correct names.

1 _Katie_ plays tennis.
2 _____ watches tennis.
3 _____ plays football.
4 _____ often goes out at weekends.

10 Work in pairs. Use the cues to make sentences about Josh and Katie.

A: *Josh often watches football on TV.*
B: *Katie never watches TV.*

Josh	Katie
1 often / watch football games on TV	1 never / watch TV
2 sometimes / go to the cinema	2 often / go to the disco
3 usually / go shopping at the weekend	3 sometimes / go shopping on Saturday
4 never / do his homework	4 always / do her homework

11 Use the cues to say true things about your life.

I usually start school at 8 a.m. ...

- start school at 8 a.m. / do my homework / relax at home
- go shopping on Saturday / do my homework / listen to my parents
- listen to pop music / go running / go to discos

TRADITIONS

Report from Australia

Martu lands

(1.33)

7 a.m. It is very hot and we are in a Land Rover. Yunkurra Taylor, seventeen, has got rock music on his MP3 player. We see a wild camel! We follow it and the men hunt the camel with guns. I am here in the desert of Western Australia with the Martu people. There are 1000 Martu in a very big area – it is the size of Greece! They speak five Aboriginal languages, like Manyjilyjarra and English is their second language. They live in small villages, like Jigalong and Parnngurr.

Yunkurra's group comes from Parnngurr – it has modern houses, a school, a clinic with a nurse and a shop.
The Martu people still have a traditional lifestyle – Martu artists paint beautiful pictures and the Martu get food from the desert. The women and children usually hunt lizards and collect fruit. The men usually hunt animals, like kangaroos, birds and wild camels.
8 p.m. We are at our camp in the desert. We make a fire and cook the camel meat. Yunkurra's dad shares the meat with the people. Then people tell stories, sing songs and Yunkurra's uncle plays the didgeridoo.
Now, the Martu people do not use boomerangs and they live in modern houses but their lives are very different from the lives of white Australians.

Warm Up

1 **Find these things (1-3) in pictures (a-e).**

1 A **didgeridoo** is a traditional musical instrument of the Australian Aborigines.
2 A **boomerang** is a traditional Aboriginal weapon to hunt wild animals.
3 This is a traditional Aboriginal **painting** of a lizard.

Reading

2 SKILLS BUILDER 7 **Use the strategies to read the article and choose one of the titles.**

a Small village life in Australia
b A traditional lifestyle
c Australian animals
d Hunting and collecting food

3 **Read the text again. Are these sentences true (T) or false (F)?**

1 The Martu people are Australian. *T*
2 The Martu haven't got modern technology.
3 They live in a small area.
4 The Martu people speak five different languages.
5 The village of Parnngurr has got a clinic.
6 Men hunt wild animals.

4 **Read the text again. Find four traditional things and four 'modern' things about the Martu's lifestyle.**

They make fires and cook meat on them. They have a clinic in the village.

5 **Look at the Sentence Builder. How do you say *like* in the sentence in your language? Find one more example of *like* in red in the text.**

> **Sentence Builder** *like* for examples
>
> 1 The men usually hunt animals, **like** kangaroos.
> 2 They live in small villages, **like** Jigalong.

LANGUAGE CHOICE 16

6 **Join the sentences with *like*.**

1 The Martu people play musical instruments. They play the didgeridoo.
   The Martu people play musical instruments, like the didgeridoo.
2 At school they play sports. They play football.
3 The men hunt animals. They hunt wild camels.
4 They use modern technology. They use MP3 players and mobile phones.
5 Martu artists paint pictures of animals. They paint lizards, kangaroos and birds.

Listening

7 1.34 1.35 **Listen to a talk about the Martu people and read the text from line 7. List six factual mistakes in the talk.**

1   *There are ~~2000~~ Martu in a very big area – 1000*

8 **Vocabulary Look at the Word Builder. Complete the table with words in blue from the text.**

Word Builder Plurals

Regular

+ *s*   house *houses*   village ¹*villages*
        bird ²_____
+ *es* bus *buses*   church *churches*
+ *ies* party *parties*   family *families*
        story ³_____

Irregular

life *lives*   man ⁴_____   woman ⁵_____
child ⁶_____   person ⁷_____

---

9 1.36 **Pronunciation Listen and repeat the plurals.**

➝ LANGUAGE CHOICE 17: VOCABULARY PRACTICE

10 **Complete the sentences with singular or plural nouns.**

1   Wild *kangaroos* live in the desert. (kangaroo)
2   There is a _____ in Parnngurr. (school)
3   My _____ is very exciting. (life)
4   That _____ hunts wild camels. (man)
5   The _____ collect fruit. (woman)
6   In the evening, they tell _____ . (story)

Your Choice

11 **Choose one of the people (a–c). Complete the sentences about their lifestyles.**

a   a teenager from London
b   a Martu teenager
c   a super-rich teenager

1   In the morning, I _____ .
2   In the evening, I _____ .
3   On Saturdays, I _____ .
4   I sometimes _____ .
5   I never _____ .

12 **Work in pairs. Read out your sentences. Guess the teenager (a–c).**

In the morning, I go to get water. Then I have breakfast at the camp.

No Comment

'We live with the land but the white man lives off it.'

Tom Dystra, Aboriginal man

GRAMMAR
MODERN LIFE

Today, Robert Evans talks to Christie, an eighteen-year-old student from Boulder University, about her lifestyle. (1.37)

R: Do you like student life, Christie?
C: Yes, I do. I like reading books and studying.
R: Where do you study?
C: Usually, I study at home but I sometimes take my laptop to a café.
R: How often do you go online?
C: I'm always online. I write a blog, I buy things, I watch films ...
R: How does the internet help you in your studies?
C: I find information on the Net.
R: How do your friends contact you?
C: We go on Facebook or Skype. We share music and read our blogs.
R: Your mother is a teacher. Does she use technology at work?
C: Yes, she does. She makes presentations for her classes.
R: And your family? Do they work with computers?
C: My father does but my brother, Brian, doesn't. He's an artist. He hates technology – he hasn't got a mobile phone!

Warm Up

1 Read the interview above with a student. How does Christie use modern technology?

Present Simple: questions

2 Complete the questions and short answers with *do* or *does*.

Questions
What do I read on the internet?
How often ¹ _*do*_ you **go** online?
² _____ she **use** technology at work?
Does he **work** with computers?
³ _____ the internet **help** you in your studies?
Where do we **use** technology?
Do you and your friends **chat** online?
How ⁴ _____ they **contact** you?
Short answers
Yes, I/you/we/they ⁵ _____ .
No, I/you/we/they **don't**.
Yes, he/she/it ⁶ _____ .
No, he/she/it **doesn't**.

3 Use the cues and the table in Exercise 2 to make questions. Then ask the questions in pairs. Give true short answers.

1 you / play computer games?
A: *Do you play computer games?*
B: *Yes, I do.*
2 your parents / write blogs?
3 you / read books?
4 your English teacher / use technology in class?
5 your grandmother / use the internet?

4 Use the cues to make questions. Then ask and answer the questions in pairs.

1 When / your parents / watch TV?
A: *When do your parents watch TV?*
B: *My parents watch TV in the evenings.*
2 What / your mother / buy online?
3 What films / you / watch online?
4 How / you / contact your friends?
5 What websites / your friends / visit regularly?
6 How often / your family / chat online?

⤳ LANGUAGE CHOICE 18

Grammar Alive Asking about habits

5 (1.38) Listen to the interview with Brian, Christie's brother. Write down the questions for these answers.

1 _Do you use a computer?_ No, I don't.
2 _____ Yes, I do.
3 _____ I don't phone them.
4 _____ We talk.

6 Use the cues and your own ideas to prepare questions for your partner.

Where do you meet your friends?
• where / meet your friends?
• what / do online? • write a blog?
• how often / chat online? • send texts?

7 Work in pairs. Ask and answer the questions from Exercise 6.

Speaking Workshop 1

1 `1.39` **DVD 1** **Listen or watch** ➡ SKILLS BUILDER 1 **Use the strategies to listen to or watch the dialogue. Answer the question below. What is the dialogue in photo a about?**

a Bob's interests and free time activities
b his lifestyle and habits
c his personal information (e.g. name/age/abilities)

2 `1.39` **DVD 1** **Listen or watch** **Listen to or watch the dialogue again. Are the sentences true (T) or false (F)?**

1 Bob and Gary are friends. *T*
2 Bob often goes canoeing.
3 Dave is the manager of the canoe club.
4 Michelle is Gary's teacher.
5 Gary and Bob like Michelle.

3 `1.40` **Look at the Talk Builder. Complete the dialogues. Listen and check your answers.**

see   bye   this   nice   ~~how~~   there

Talk Builder Meeting people

1 **Meet a person you know**
A: Good morning, Gary, ¹ ___*how*___ are you?
B: I'm fine, thanks.

2 **Introductions**
A: ² _____ is my friend, Bob.
B: This is Michelle.

3 **Meet a new person**
A: Hello, Bob. My name's Dave.
B: Hi there. ³ _____ to meet you.

A: Hi ⁴ _____ .
B: Hi, good to meet you.

4 **Say goodbye**
A: ⁵ _____ you later!
B: ⁶ _____ , Gary! Have a good time!
A: And you.

➡ SKILLS BUILDER 29

4 `1.41` **Pronunciation Listen and repeat the expressions.**

5 **Choose the correct replies.**

1 Good morning, Pete. How are you?
a Good to meet you. ⓑ Fine thanks.
c See you later.
2 Tom, this is Karen.
a Hi there. b Yes, Karen. c Thanks.
3 See you later.
a Hi there. b And you. c Bye.
4 Have a good time.
a Fine thanks. b And you. c Hi there.

6 **Speaking Work in pairs. Practise the dialogues in Exercise 5. Change the names.**

7 **Work in groups. Imagine you go to a new sports club. Act out dialogues.**

➡ SKILLS BUILDER 29

1 **Invent a character. Make notes about these things:**

• his/her name and age
• where he/she is from
• his/her sporting abilities

2 **Imagine you are the manager of the club. Think of questions to ask the character.**

How old are you?

3 ➡ SKILLS BUILDER 30 **Practise saying phrases from the Talk Builder.**

4 **Work in groups of three (students A–C). Take turns to act out the dialogues on page 116.**

A: *Good morning, Tina. How are you?*
B: *Fine thanks.*

Writing Workshop 1

¹Hi Sandra,

A How are you and your family? ²We're fine. Perth is great and I really like the lifestyle.

B Perth is a big city in Australia but it's different from London and it's very relaxed. We've got a house with a swimming pool and it's near the beach. On Saturday and Sunday, I go swimming and surfing. Surfing is great!

C I go to Shenton High School – it's a big school but Australian people are friendly. I like the school but it's hard work – I've got eight classes every day. In the afternoon, I play football or basketball. When I get home, I swim or do my homework – we have ³TWO HOURS of homework! Then I play computer games and chat with my friends online.

D Is it cold in London? It is usually horrible in February ⁴!!!!!!!

⁵Write soon.

Christine

① **Read the letter and answer these questions.**

1 Where does Christine live?
   Christine lives in Perth.
2 Where is Christine from?
3 What are the good things about Perth?
4 What does she do at the weekend?
5 What is hard work for her?
6 What does she do in the evening?

Text Builder

② **Match the paragraphs in the letter (A-D) with the headings (1-4).**

1 life at school *C*   3 ending
2 introduction   4 life in Perth

③ **⟳ SKILLS BUILDER 8 Use the information in the Skills Builder to match the examples of informal style in blue (1-5) in the letter with these things (a-b):**

a punctuation: CAPITAL LETTERS, exclamation marks !!!!!!, contractions (can't)
b informal expressions: to start a letter, to finish a letter

④ **Look at the Sentence Builder. How do you say the words in bold in your language?**

Sentence Builder *and/or*

1 In the afternoon, I play football **or** basketball.
2 When I get home, I swim **or** do my homework.
3 On Saturday and Sunday, we go swimming **and** surfing.
4 I study maths, computer science, English **and** Japanese.
5 I play computer games **and** chat with my friends online.

⟳ SKILLS BUILDER 15

⑤ **Complete the sentences with *and/or*.**

1 I have breakfast __and__ listen to the radio.
2 I cycle _____ walk to school.
3 On Mondays, we have maths _____ English.
4 I have lunch at school _____ at home.
5 In the afternoon, I play tennis _____ golf.
6 In the evening, I eat dinner _____ watch TV.

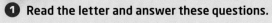

⑥ **Write a personal letter to a friend.**

⟳ SKILLS BUILDER 16

1 Choose a place and imagine you live there. Write notes about these things:

   • your new house   • the city   • school
   • after school and weekend

2 Use your notes to write the letter.

3 Give your letter to your partner to read.

⑦ **Work in groups. Tell the class about your partner's new life.**

Ivan now lives in Los Angeles. He goes surfing after school.

LEARNING LINKS: 1 Sound Choice 1 → MyLab / Workbook page 19. Choose three pronunciation activities to do.
2 Check Your Progress 1 → MyLab / Workbook page 20. Complete the **Module Diary**.

2 AT HOME

Objectives: **Listen, read** and **talk about** homes; **make** and **reply** to suggestions; **write** a short description of a house; **learn about** *there is/are* and *some/any* and (un)countable nouns and *a lot of/no*.

TOPIC TALK

1 Find words in the network in the photos (a–b).

2 1.42 **1.43** Listen and match the descriptions (1–2) to the rooms in the photos (a–b).

3 1.44 **1.45** Listen again to the first person. Complete the information in the network.

4 1.46 **Pronunciation** Listen and write down the words. Listen again and <u>underline</u> the main stress.

fa̱vourite, co̱mfortable

> LANGUAGE CHOICE 19:
> VOCABULARY PRACTICE

5 Work in groups. Use the network to talk about *your* home.

My home

Our ¹*house/flat* has got ² _three_ bedrooms.
My favourite room is ³_____ .
It has got modern ⁴*furniture/floors*.
It's got two ⁵_____ and a ⁶_____ .
It's a great place to ⁷*study/relax*.
I like my home because it's ⁸*comfortable/modern/ tidy/light*.

Rooms
the bathroom, dining room, hall, kitchen, living room, toilet
my bedroom, room

Furniture
armchair, bed, bookshelf, chair, cupboard, desk, sofa, table, wardrobe

- -

door, floor, shower, toilet, walls, window
carpet, curtains, lamp, mirror, picture, plant, poster
computer, cooker, dishwasher, fridge, microwave, oven
stereo system, TV, washing machine

23

a

Warm Up

1 Look at the photos (a–c). What can you say about their owners' lifestyle, hobbies and interests?

The person in room b is a girl. She likes pink. She is interested in pop music.

2 Read two people's answers to a questionnaire about their rooms. Which photos (a–c) show Lena's and Justin's rooms?

3 Which room do you like? Why?

there is/are, some/any

4 Complete the sentences from the text with *is, are, isn't* or *aren't*. How do you say the sentences in your language?

Affirmative	
There [1] *is* a stereo system.	
There [2]_____ two guitars in my room.	
Negative	
There [3]_____ a wardrobe.	
There [4]_____ any CDs.	
Questions	**Short answers**
[5]_____ **there** a TV in your room?	Yes, **there** [8]_____ .
	No, **there** [9]_____ .
[6]_____ **there** any posters on the walls?	Yes, **there** [10]_____ .
	No, **there** [11]_____ .
What furniture [7]_____ **there** in your room?	

5 Read the sentences (1–3) and complete the rules below with *some* and *any*.

1 There are **some** bookshelves.
2 There aren't **any** books.
3 Are there **any** pictures on the walls?

- We use _____ in questions and negative sentences.
- We use _____ in affirmative sentences.

My room [1.47]

Can you describe your room?

Lena: It's dark because there is only one small window but it's very big.

Justin: My room's big and light.

What furniture is there in your room?

Lena: There is a big bed, a desk, a wardrobe and a chair. There are some bookshelves, too. And there is my pet tarantula.

Justin: There is only my bed, a desk and a chair. There isn't a wardrobe, I keep my clothes on the shelves. There aren't any CDs – I buy my music online. There are two guitars – I am in a rock band.

Is there a TV in your room?

Lena: No, there isn't. And there isn't a computer. I don't like technology.

Justin: Yes, there is. There is also a stereo system and a computer.

Are there any posters on the walls?

Lena: No, there aren't. There aren't any posters but there are some photos – photography is my hobby.

Justin: Yes, there are. There are posters of *Kings of Leon* and *The Killers* – they're my favourite groups.

Practice

6 Complete the questions about someone's room with *Is* or *Are?*

1 ___Is___ there a carpet?
2 _____ there a sofa in the room?
3 _____ there any curtains?
4 _____ there a computer on the desk?
5 _____ there any CDs or DVDs in the room?
6 _____ there any bookshelves?
7 _____ there a lamp on the desk?
8 What pictures _____ there on the walls?

⇢ LANGUAGE CHOICE 20

7 Complete the dialogue with *some* or *any.*

A: Are there ¹___any___ computers in your English classroom?
B: No, there aren't ²_____ computers. There are ³_____ desks and chairs and an old TV.
A: Are there ⁴_____ bookshelves?
B: Yes, there are. There are ⁵_____ English dictionaries and encyclopedias on them. But there aren't ⁶_____ interesting books.
A: Are there ⁷_____ posters or photos?
B: Yes, there are ⁸_____ maps and ⁹_____ photos of London.

⇢ LANGUAGE CHOICE 21

8 Work in pairs. Choose one of the photos (a–c). Ask and answer the questions from Exercise 6 to guess your partner's photo.

Are there any bookshelves?

Grammar Alive Describing rooms

9 〔1.48〕 Listen to two descriptions of rooms. Tick the right boxes in the table.

	Ben's room	Sharon's room
carpet	✓	
computer		
wardrobe		
desk		
posters		

10 Work in pairs. Use the cues below to ask about your partner's room.

A: *Is there a carpet in your room?*
B: *Yes, there is a white carpet.*
A: *Are there any pictures on the walls?*
B: *Yes, there are. There are some posters of rock bands.*

carpet   curtains   wardrobe   desk
pictures   lamps   chairs   armchairs
musical instruments   stereo system
computer   bookshelves   plants   books

11 Remember your partner's answers from Exercise 10 and describe his/her room. He/She corrects your description.

A: *Your room is small. There is a blue carpet.*
B: *No, there is a white carpet.*

SMART HOME

Warm Up

1 Look at the things (a–d) in the photos. What machines have you got in your home? What is your favourite machine?

My favourite machine at home is the fridge!

Reading

2 Read the text. Match the descriptions (1–8) with the machines (a–g). There is one extra description.

1 cleans the floors *e*
2 looks after animals
3 orders food on the internet
4 controls the temperature of the water and has a TV
5 cooks dinner automatically
6 you can do exercise on it
7 talks to the driver
8 looks after old people

a Wakamaru domestic robot
b intelligent oven
c exercise bike with computer
d PIVO 2 car
e Homebot
f intelligent shower
g intelligent fridge

3 What things do you like about Michiko's home?

4 Vocabulary Look at the Word Builder. Are the sentences true (T) or false (F) about Michiko and her home? How do you say the words in **bold** in your language?

> **Word Builder** Multi-part verbs (1)
>
> 1 I **wake up** at six o'clock. *F*
> 2 I **get up** at five past seven.
> 3 I **go out** at eight o'clock.
> 4 Homebot **looks after** my mother.
> 5 I **get back** home at six o'clock.
> 6 I **go to bed** at eleven o'clock.
> 7 I **go to sleep** at eleven o'clock.

➜ LANGUAGE CHOICE 22: VOCABULARY PRACTICE

A DAY IN THE LIFE OF ...

A HOME OF THE FUTURE.

Dr Michiko Ishiguru, describes a typical day at her smart home in Tokyo. 〔1.49〕

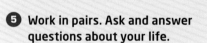

a *Intelligent fridge*

7.00 I wake up. The lights are on and I can hear my favourite music. The curtains open automatically, too – it is cold outside but my bedroom is warm.

7.05 I get up and go to the bathroom. I watch the TV in my intelligent shower – it knows my favourite water temperature.

7.20 My mother and I have breakfast. We have fruit – my intelligent fridge orders food from the internet. It knows when we need food, like milk or fruit.

7.45 I program my vacuum cleaner, Homebot, to clean the floors. I put tonight's dinner in the intelligent oven. I can check the dinner with my mobile phone.

8.00 I go out. I go to work in my PIVO 2 car – it talks and gives me traffic information. My mother stays with Wakamaru, our intelligent robot. It looks after her and phones me when she is not well.

5 Work in pairs. Ask and answer questions about your life.

1 What time do you wake up?
   I usually wake up at seven o'clock.
2 What time do you get up?
3 What time do you usually go out in the morning?
4 When do you usually get back home?
5 Do you ever look after a person in your family (e.g. young brother or sister)?
6 When do you go to bed and when do you go to sleep?

d *Wakamaru*

b *Homebot*

18.00 I get back home. I ride my exercise bike – it has got a computer. I can choose different routes and today I go cycling in the Alps!

19.00 Dinner is ready in the intelligent oven. Great!

20.00 We watch a film on the home cinema in the living room.

23.30 I go to bed and read an e-book. Then I go to sleep.

c *Intelligent shower*

Writing

6 **Read the description of Michiko's house. What two *new* machines does she mention?**

My house is very modern. In my bedroom, I've got a stereo system and a TV. In the kitchen there is an intelligent fridge. On the kitchen table there is an automatic coffee maker. In the living room, I've got an exercise bike with a computer and there is a home cinema on the wall. The home computer is in the hall – it controls things in the house like the lights and the temperature. I can phone it when I'm not at home. I can check the house when I am at work or at friends' houses.

7 **Look at the Sentence Builder. How do you say the words in red in your language? Find more examples of *in/on/at* in the description from Exercise 6.**

> **Sentence Builder**
> **Prepositions of place: *in/on/at***
>
> **in**: I am in the classroom. My mobile phone is in my bag. Rome is in Italy.
> **on**: My book is on the table. I keep my clothes on the shelves. There are pictures on the wall.
> **at**: I am at school now. My sister is at a party. My dad is at the shops.
>
> ➡ SKILLS BUILDER 17

↘ LANGUAGE CHOICE 23

8 **Complete the sentences with *in*, *on* or *at*.**

1 When I am __at__ home, I often use the computer _____ my room.
2 There isn't any food _____ the fridge but there's some fruit _____ the table.
3 There is a blue carpet _____ the floor _____ the living room.
4 I often sing _____ the shower.
5 I've got posters of stars _____ the walls _____ my bedroom.
6 My mum is _____ work and my dad is _____ the shops.

9 **Choose one of the houses (a–d). Write eight sentences about it.**

a my grandmother's house.
b my house
c a hi-tech house
d my dream house

10 **Work in pairs. Ask and answer questions about your houses.**

A: *What is there in the living room?*
B: *In the living room there is a home cinema …*

Your Choice

> **No Comment**
>
> 'There's no place like home.'
>
> *English proverb*

GRAMMAR
MICRO HOMES

Warm Up

1 Look at the house in the photo. Guess what rooms, furniture and machines are in it.

2 Read the interview and check your guesses.

LIVES (1.50)

We talk to Thomas Meier from Munich Technical University about his micro home.

Q: Is this house different from your family home?

TM: Yes, there are no carpets and there is a lot of metal and glass. There is a table and chairs but I haven't got any armchairs. I've got electricity but there's no gas. In the kitchen there is a microwave and a small fridge but there isn't an oven.

Q: How many rooms have you got there?

TM: There is one room and a mini-bathroom with a shower.

Q: How much space is there in the house?

TM: There isn't much space. But there is some space for cups and plates. I've got a lot of books but there are no bookshelves!

Q: Do you like this house?

TM: Yes, it is comfortable. But I've got a lot of friends and I can only invite three people!

Countable/Uncountable nouns and *a lot of/no*

3 Complete the lists with more nouns from the text. Then complete the rules below with *countable* or *uncountable*.

> **countable nouns** (you can count the things):
> *room (rooms), carpet (carpets) …*
> **uncountable nouns** (you can't count the thing):
> *space, metal, …*

1 _____ nouns are always singular.
2 _____ nouns can be singular or plural.
3 _____ nouns don't take *a/an*.
4 _____ nouns never go with numbers (one, two, …)

---

4 Read the sentences (1-6) from the text. Which expressions in **bold** do we use with:

a plural countable nouns?
b uncountable nouns?

1 **How many** rooms have you got? *a*
2 **How much** space is there in the house?
3 I've got **a lot of** books.
4 There is **a lot of** metal.
5 There are **no** carpets.
6 There's **no** gas.

5 Complete the interview with *how much, how many, a lot of, no* or *a/an*.

A: ¹_____ furniture is there in your room?
B: I've got ²_____ big desk and there are always ³_____ notebooks on it. There isn't ⁴_____ armchair in my room because I've got ⁵_____ space for it. There are ⁶_____ computers in my room – I use my mother's computer.
A: ⁷_____ books are there?
B: I'm interested in history and I've got ⁸_____ history books.
A: ⁹_____ time do you spend in your room?
B: I love my room and I spend ¹⁰_____ time here.

↳ LANGUAGE CHOICE 24

Grammar Alive
Talking about quantity

6 (1.51) Listen to the dialogue. Use the cues and *a lot of* or *no* to make true sentences about who/what there is in Joanna's home.

There are a lot of girls.

- girls • boys • pizzas
- water • cola • juice

7 Use the cues below and *how much/how many* to ask and answer questions about your room.

A: *How many books are there in your room?*
B: *There are no books in my room. I don't like reading.*

- books • pens • money • CDs
- notebooks • pencils • light • space

Speaking Workshop 2

1 **Vocabulary** Look at the photo and the vocabulary box below. Make guesses about the feelings of the people.

Zoe is worried.

Feelings
angry, bored, excited, happy, hungry, nervous, sad, scared, thirsty, tired, unhappy, worried

2 1.52 DVD 2 **Listen or watch** Listen to or watch the dialogue. Check your guesses.

Emma is thirsty.

3 1.52 DVD 2 **Listen or watch** Listen to or watch the dialogue again. Order these events.

a Emma gets some orange juice.
b Zoe can't find her laptop.
c Emma goes on the computer.
d Their mum comes in and is happy with Emma.
e Emma lays the table for dinner. *7*
f Emma gets a message from her mum. *1*
g Emma plays a computer game.
h Zoe wants to study for an exam.

4 Look at the Talk Builder. How do you say the words in bold in your language?

Talk Builder Suggestions

Suggest
1 **Why don't you** play a computer game?
2 **Let's** start.
Accept
3 **All right**. **Okay**. **Good idea**.
Reject
4 **No**, … (I don't want to/I'm tired).
5 **I'm not sure**.

➔ SKILLS BUILDER 31

5 1.53 **Pronunciation** Listen and repeat the replies.

6 **Speaking** Work in pairs. Use the cues below to act out dialogues.

Feelings:
I'm bored, tired, hungry, thirsty, sad, worried, angry.
Suggestions:
Why don't you … go out, read a book, get a drink, watch a film, go shopping, go to bed, talk to a friend, talk to your dad/mum/boyfriend/girlfriend?
Let's … play a computer game, go out, have lunch, go to the cinema, go to a café, play tennis, watch that film, watch TV.
Replies:
Okay./No, I'm tired, I haven't got any money, I haven't got time, it's very hot/cold, I don't like it, I don't want to.

A: *I'm hungry.*
B: *Let's have lunch.*
A: *Okay.*

7 Work in pairs. Act out a situation.

➔ SKILLS BUILDER 31

1 **Choose one of the situations (a–c).**
a you are at your grandparents' house with your brother/sister and there is no internet
b you are in a hotel on holiday with a friend and you are hungry and thirsty
c you are at school with your partner and you have some free time – you are worried about your exams

2 **Think of suggestions of things to do.**
   Buy some water. Go to a café.

3 **Work in pairs. Act out the situations.**
   A: *I'm very thirsty because it's hot.*
   B: *Why don't you …?*

8 Tell the class your suggestions for the situations.

a *Let's go to the hotel café for a drink.*
b *Why don't you play football?*

Language Review Modules 1 and 2

① **Interests/Home/Feelings** Choose the correct words to complete the sentences.

A: On Saturday, I often [1]*do/go* swimming and running and then I'm [2]*tired/scared*. I [3]*use/play* the internet a lot: I often [4]*chat/watch* with my friends online.
B: Our [5]*bathroom/kitchen* has got a table and two big windows – it's very [6]*light/tidy*.
C: I'm [7]*bored/angry* when my brother [8]*plays/listens* to music on my MP3 player.
D: Are you [9]*hungry/thirsty*? There is some cold water in the [10]*fridge/wardrobe*. **/10**

② **Prepositions of place/Multi-part verbs (1)/*like/and*, or** Complete the text with *at, in, on, out, like, and, or, up, to* or *back*.

11 In the morning, I get _____ at seven o'clock. I have breakfast and I go _____ at 7.30.
12 I am _____ school for seven _____ eight hours.
13 I get _____ home at about five o'clock. Then I usually relax _____ my room.
14 I like my room: there are photos of my favourite football stars, _____ Rooney and Ronaldo, _____ the walls.
15 In the evening, I have dinner _____ do my homework. I go _____ bed at ten o'clock. **/5**

③ **Present Simple** Complete the sentences with the correct form of the verbs in brackets.

A: What [16]_____ (you / do) in your free time?
B: I [17]_____ (read) books. My friends often [18]_____ (go) to the cinema but I [19]_____ (not go) with them. I [20]_____ (watch) DVDs at home.
A: [21]_____ (you / like) sport?
B: No, I don't but my boyfriend [22]_____ (play) basketball and football. He [23]_____ (not like) reading.
A: [24]_____ (he / watch) films with you?
B: Yes, he does. We [25]_____ (love) Alfred Hitchcock's films. **/10**

④ **Adverbs of frequency** Put the adverb in the correct place in the sentence.

26 We stay at home on Sunday. (often)
27 I start school at 8.30. (always)
28 My parents are tired in the evening. (usually)
29 My friends chat online in the morning. (never)
30 I am tired at school. (sometimes) **/5**

⑤ **Plural, countable and uncountable nouns** Make the nouns plural, if possible, and put the verb *be* in the correct form.

31 There _____ (not be) a lot of _____ (water) in the Sahara.
32 There _____ (be) interesting _____ (story) in this book.
33 Their three _____ (child) _____ (be) always bored. **/6**

⑥ ***there is/are, some, any, no, how much/many*** Complete the dialogue with *some, any, no, much* or *many* and put the verb *be* in the correct form.

A: How [34]_____ people are there in your class?
B: There [35]_____ (be) twenty-five boys. There aren't [36]_____ girls.
A: I'm in a school for girls. There are [37]_____ boys in my class.
A: Let's have a party in my house.
B: Good idea! How [38]_____ space have you got?
A: There [39]_____ (be) a lot of space. **/6**

⑦ **Meeting people** Complete the dialogues with the correct words.

Josh: Hi, my [40]_____ is Josh. And [41]_____ is my friend, Carl.
Karen: [42]_____ to meet you. I'm Karen.

Ann: [43]_____ are you, Karen?
Karen: I'm [44]_____ , thanks. And you?
Ann: I'm okay. Have a nice evening! **/5**

⑧ **Suggestions** Complete the gaps in the dialogue with the correct lines (a-d). There is one extra line.

A: I'm bored.
B: [45]_____
A: There aren't any films.
B: [46]_____
A: Good idea! [47]_____

a Okay. Why don't we go out?
b Let's watch TV.
c Let's go to the park.
d No, I don't like TV. **/3**

Self Assessment

1.54 Listen and check your answers. Write down your scores. Use the table to find practice exercises.

Exercise	If you need practice, go to
1	Language Choice 13, 19
2	Language Choice 16, 22, 23
3	Language Choice 14, 18
4	Language Choice 15
5	Language Choice 17
6	Language Choice 20, 21, 24
7	SB p.21 ex.3
8	SB p.29 ex.4

LEARNING LINKS: 1 Read and listen to the short story in **Culture Choice 1** on page 97. Then do a project about your home.
2 Exam Choice 1 → MyLab / Workbook pages 28-29.
3 Check Your Progress 2 → MyLab / Workbook page 30. Complete the **Module Diary**.

30

3 DOWNTOWN

Objectives: Listen, read and **talk about** going out; **ask for** and **give** information about concerts; **write** a short note; **learn about** comparative and superlative adjectives.

TOPIC TALK

1 Look at the photos (a–c) and the network. What places can you see in the photos?

a *shops*

2 `1.55` `1.56` Listen and match the people (1–3) with their favourite places (a–c).

a cafés and theatres
b clubs and outdoor markets
c art galleries and skate parks

3 `1.57` `1.58` Listen again to the first description. Complete the information in the network.

Going out

In my ¹ *town/city*, there are a lot of good
² _____ .
There aren't a lot of good ³_____ .
I love ⁴_____ and ⁵_____ .
My favourite place is a ⁶ *café/skate park/club.*
I like it because it is ⁷_____ .
I don't like our local ⁸*shopping centre/
cinema/swimming pool/club* because it's very
⁹_____ .

➜ LANGUAGE CHOICE 25:
   VOCABULARY PRACTICE

4 `1.59` Pronunciation Listen to the words below. <u>Underline</u> the words which have a silent 'r'.

<u>theatre</u>, restaurant, centre,
comfortable, modern, outdoor,
market, friendly, favourite,
galleries, park

5 Work in groups. Use the network to talk about *your* town/city.

Places
(outdoor) cafés, night clubs,
pubs, restaurants, shops,
outdoor markets,
shopping centres
art galleries, cinemas,
museums, theatres
amusement parks, skate parks,
sports centres, swimming pools

Adjectives
big, cheap, comfortable, exciting, friendly,
interesting, quiet, modern, nice, relaxed
----
boring, busy, dark, expensive, noisy, small

a Dublin

 b Prague

c New York

31

GRAMMAR
CLUBS

Warm Up

1 **Where do you go with your friends?**

We go to cafés.

> cafés   the cinema   clubs   the park
> a sports centre   a shopping centre

2 **Read two advertisements of clubs for teenagers. Which club do you like? Why?**

I like Stardust. They've got a great DJ and there is live music.

dance Fusion

Fri and Sat 8 p.m. – 1 a.m.
Tickets: £15
Hip hop, rock, house music
DJs: DJ Raven,
Big Steve
No alcohol
or smoking
No jeans
or hoods

STARDUST TEEN CLUB

Every day 3 p.m. – 11 p.m.
Tickets: £8
Live rock music on Saturdays
DJ: Chris Jones

3 **Read peoples' comments about the two clubs. Which clubs do they like?**

4 **Are there clubs for teenagers in your town? Do you like them?**

Comparatives

5 **Complete the table with correct forms of the adjectives from the text.**

	Adjective	Comparative
one syllable	nice	1 _nicer_
	old	old**er**
one syllable with a short vowel and a consonant	big	2 _____
-y at the end	busy	3 _____
	friendly	4 _____
two or more syllables	expensive	5 _____
	interesting	**more/less** interesting
	exciting	6 _____
irregular	good	7 _____
	bad	8 _____

Dance Fusion or Stardust
what do you think? 1.60

 DJ99
Dance Fusion is really cool. It is more expensive than Stardust but the music is better. It is bigger, too – there are three different rooms with hip hop, rock and house.

 outsider
Stardust is cheaper and it is better for young people. The atmosphere is more relaxed there. There are really good drinks and the food is bett than at Dance Fusion (fantastic hamburgers!!).

 poshhh
I think Stardust is less interesting. It's smaller tha Dance Fusion and the DJ is worse. Dance Fusion busier and the music is more exciting. The peopl at Dance Fusion are friendlier than at Stardust.

 qreator
I prefer Dance Fusion. The atmosphere is nicer than at Stardust – the people are older and more interesting than at Stardust. It's quieter and you can talk to your friends.

6 **Read the sentence below. Translate the word in bold into your language.**

*Dance Fusion is more expensive **than** Stardust.*

7 **Read the sentences (1-2). Put the expressions in bold on the scale.**

1 *People at Dance Fusion are **more** interesting.*
2 *Stardust is **less** interesting.*

↑ exciting
_____ interesting
interesting
_____ interesting

dance Fusion

Practice

8 Use the information from the text to complete the sentences (1-6). Use the comparative forms of the adjectives in brackets.

1 Dance Fusion is _more expensive_ than Stardust. (expensive)
2 DJs at Dance Fusion are _____ than at Stardust. (good)
3 Music at Stardust is _____ than at Dance Fusion. (exciting)
4 People at Dance Fusion are _____ than at Stardust. (old)
5 Food at Dance Fusion is _____ than at Stardust. (bad)
6 People at Dance Fusion are _____ than at Stardust. (interesting)

➡ LANGUAGE CHOICE 26

9 Look at the two clubs in the photos (a-b). Use the adjectives below to write about them.

Stardust is smaller than Dance Fusion.

modern   small   big   old   dark   nice   comfortable

10 Complete the review of two cafés with correct comparative forms of the adjectives in brackets.

I think Coco is better than Mocha. First, Mocha is ¹ _smaller_ (small) and there are only five tables. Coco is ² _____ (big) and it's in a ³ _____ (nice) area – it's in a park and you can eat outdoors in the summer. I don't like the waiters at Mocha – they are ⁴ _____ (old) and ⁵ _____ (friendly) than at Coco. The drinks in Coco are ⁶ _____ (interesting) and ⁷ _____ (expensive) than at Mocha – I love their hot chocolate!

➡ LANGUAGE CHOICE 27

Grammar Alive
Comparing places

11 1.61 Listen to the dialogue. Put a tick (✓) in the correct place in the column. Then compare the two cafés.

Ristretto is nicer than Samba.

	Ristretto	Samba
nice	✓	
big		
busy		
expensive		
good		

12 Work in pairs. Take turns to make sentences about two snack bars: Jake's Burgers and Green Café. Use the cues below.

Jake's Burgers is older than Green Café. The chairs at Jake's Burgers are more comfortable than at Green Café.

	Jake's Burgers	Green Café
old	✓	
expensive		✓
chairs – comfortable	✓	
tables – big	✓	
coffee – good		✓
food – interesting		✓
quiet		✓

13 Use the cues and your own ideas to compare two places to meet in your area (clubs/bars/cafés).

Metro Café is bigger and more comfortable than Papaya.

big   modern   friendly   comfortable
quiet   busy   cheap

SKILLS
FREE FUN

Covent Garden

Warm Up

1 Which of the things below are sometimes or always free in London? Guess the answers.

concerts   night clubs   museums
art galleries   professional football
games (e.g. Spurs and Chelsea)
sightseeing   running and skating
films   street performers
sports centres   plays

Reading

2 Read the website and check your guesses from Exercise 1.

3 Read the website again. Complete the notes.

1 Free music at: *the National Theatre, the HMV Music Store* , *Covent Garden Market*
2 Street performers at: _____
3 Exhibits in the Science Museum: *modern technology, _____ , interactive exhibits about biology*
4 Good modern art at: _____
5 Nelson's Column is in: _____
6 You can go running in: _____

4 Work in pairs. Tell your partner which activities from the website are interesting for you. Give your reasons.

A: *I like the street performers because I love music and theatre.*
B: *For me, the Science Museum is interesting because I love science.*

LONDON FOR FREE ⟨1.62⟩

London is expensive but you can have a lot of fun for free. Don't stay at home! Go out and enjoy the city!

There are free concerts at the <u>National Theatre</u> and you can sometimes listen to famous pop groups at the <u>HMV Music Store</u>. People under twenty-five can get free tickets at two hundred London theatres. In the summer, there are free concerts, plays and films at the *More London Free Festival*. There are great street performers, like musicians and acrobats at <u>Covent Garden Market</u> in the evenings.

A lot of London's museums and art galleries are free. At <u>the Science Museum</u> you can see modern technology and old machines. There are great interactive exhibitions, like *Who am I?*, an exhibition about biology. <u>Tate Modern</u> has a good collection of modern art and fantastic exhibitions.

5 Vocabulary Look at the Word Builder and the words in red in the London website. Complete the sentences.

Word Builder Verbs and prepositions

1 Don't **stay** _at_ home!
2 You can **listen** _____ famous pop groups.
3 Millions of tourists **come** _____ London every year.
4 **Go** _____ Trafalgar Square.
5 **Walk** _____ Buckingham Palace.
6 The Queen **lives** _____ the palace.
7 **Look** _____ the old objects and the cool clothes.
8 They **go** _____ the streets of London.

➤ LANGUAGE CHOICE 28: VOCABULARY PRACTICE

6 Complete the description with verbs from the Word Builder.

1.7 million people [1] _live_ in Barcelona but millions of tourists [2]_____ to our city every year. Barcelona is a great place to visit but [3]_____ at a hotel in the centre. In the morning, [4]_____ to the old city and visit the art galleries. In the evening, [5]_____ around the streets near the Rambla – there's an outdoor market and street performers. At night, [6]_____ to some good music or dance at a club.

Science Museum

Millions of tourists come to London every year to see the sights. Go to Trafalgar Square and see Nelson's Column. Then walk to Buckingham Palace – the Queen lives in the palace when she is in London. Go to Portobello Market at the weekend. It is not cheap but it is a great place to visit – you can look at the old objects and the cool clothes there.

Sports centres in London are not free but you can go running in parks like Hyde Park. And on Friday evenings, 5000 people put on their roller skates and go around the streets of London.

Rollerskating

Listening

7 1.63 1.64 → SKILLS BUILDER 2 **Use the strategies to listen to the recorded information and complete the sentences.**

The National Theatre
There are free concerts at [1] *a quarter to six* every day but not at the weekend. There are [2] _____ buses to the theatre.

Tate Modern
It opens at [3] _____ o'clock in the morning and closes at [4] _____ o'clock. On Fridays and [5] _____ , it closes at ten o'clock at night.

St Paul's Cathedral
It is open for sightseeing from [6] _____ to four o'clock in the afternoon. There are free concerts on [7] _____ afternoons.

Hyde Park
Hyde Park opens at [8] _____ o'clock in the morning every day until midnight. You can go [9] _____ or cycling and you can play [10] _____ in the park in the summer.

8 **Look at the words in red from Exercise 7. Complete the Sentence Builder with the words that follow them.**

> **Sentence Builder** Time prepositions
>
> **in:** [1] *the morning* , [2] _____ , the evening, the spring, [3] _____ , the autumn, the winter
> **on:** Mondays, Wednesdays, [4] _____ , Thursday mornings, Saturday afternoons, [5] _____
> **at:** [6] _____ , [7] _____ , half-past six, seven o'clock, [8] _____ , [9] _____

→ LANGUAGE CHOICE 29

9 **Complete the description with time prepositions.**

The museum opens [1] *at* nine o'clock and closes [2] _____ the evening [3] _____ six o'clock. [4] _____ Fridays and Saturdays, it closes [5] _____ eight o'clock [6] _____ night. [7] _____ Saturday mornings, there are free films. [8] _____ the summer, there are free concerts in the garden. They are [9] _____ the weekend, [10] _____ Saturday evenings.

10 **Choose two of the activities below (a-f). Write notes about the activities in your town or city.**

a sightseeing/places to visit
b music
c films/plays
d museums/galleries
e sport/exercise
f markets

Prague:
Charles Bridge - summer evenings: street performers
American Centre - free films in English – Thursdays 6 p.m.
Sightseeing - Old Town, Charles Bridge, John Lennon Wall

11 **Work in groups. Tell your partners about the activities.**

Go to Charles Bridge and listen to the free concerts. They are at seven o'clock in the evening.

> **No Comment**
>
> 'When a man is tired of London, he is tired of life.'
>
> Samuel Johnson, English writer

Your Choice

GRAMMAR
SKATERS

Warm Up

1 Read the text. Is the South Bank an interesting place? Why?

2 What place in your area can you call 'your second home'?

The South Bank is one of the busiest places in London. It has got museums and theatres but it also has the oldest and the most famous skate park in London, with lots of concrete steps and artistic graffiti.
There are always a lot of people here – tourists and Londoners come to watch. The skaters here can do the most difficult skating tricks. But the skate park welcomes even the least experienced skaters.
'I'm not a great skater but here I can learn the coolest tricks from the best people in the world. Everybody is really friendly, we are a big family and this is our second home.' says sixteen-year-old Ben.
The London City Council plan to close the South Bank skate park and build shops there. But for now, skaters can still use the nicest skate spot in the city.

[1.65]

Superlatives

3 Complete the table with correct forms of adjectives from the text.

	Adjective	Superlative
one syllable	old cool nice	1 _the oldest_ 2 _____ 3 _____
one syllable with a short vowel and a consonant	big	the big**gest**
-*y* at the end	busy	4 _____
two or more syllables	famous difficult	5 _____ 6 _____
irregular	good bad	7 _____ the worst

↘ LANGUAGE CHOICE 30

4 Put these two phrases in the correct places on the line below.

the most friendly   *the least friendly*

– _____ friendly _____ +

5 Complete the sentences with the superlative form of the adjectives in brackets.

The South Bank is ¹ _the coolest_ (cool) place I know. It's got ² _____ (nice) atmosphere in town. Some of my ³ _____ (good) friends skate here. Maybe this spot is not ⁴ _____ (beautiful) place in London but it is ⁵ _____ (exciting).

6 Complete the sentences with *most* or *least*.

1 London is the _most_ exciting city in the world.
2 The centre is the _____ quiet area in a city.
3 Manhattan is the _____ relaxing part of New York.
4 Restaurants in the city centre are usually the _____ expensive.
5 Hyde Park is the _____ famous park in London.

Grammar Alive Talking about cities

7 *[1.66]* Listen to three people offering their suggestions for the UK's best city. Why do they like their cities?

Edinburgh: *has got the best night clubs.*
Cardiff:
Cambridge:

8 Work in pairs. Use the cues to make sentences about these towns and respond to them.

1 Kraków - old university in Poland (→ Warsaw University - good)
  A: *Kraków has the oldest university in Poland.*
  B: *Okay, but Warsaw University is the best.*
2 Athens - old town in Europe (→ Rome - beautiful)
3 Hollywood - famous town in the world (→ Buenos Aires - exciting)
4 Tokyo - big city in the world (→ London - cool)
5 New York - good restaurants in the world (→ Paris - good shops)

9 Think of the towns in your country. Use superlatives to make sentences about them.

Brno is the most beautiful town in the Czech Republic.

big   nice   expensive   beautiful
dangerous   old   exciting   modern

Speaking Workshop 3

1 Look at the photo. Where is it: a) a cinema b) a ticket office c) a club?

2 `1.67` `DVD 3` Listen or watch Listen to or watch the dialogue. Check your guess from Exercise 1. Complete the information in the table.

Concert	Day/Time	Price of tickets
Big rock concert	¹ *Saturday*	from £35 to ²£____
Comedy and music night	³_____	⁴£____
Thames Festival	⁵_____ at ⁶_____ o'clock	free

3 `1.67` `DVD 3` Listen or watch Listen to or watch the dialogue again. Match the information with the people in the photos (Patsy (P), Gary (G) and the ticket agent (TA).

1 gives information about shows in London *TA*
2 is very interested in the rock concert
3 asks for information about cheaper shows
4 is interested in the comedy show
5 is worried about the price of the tickets
6 asks for information about the free festival
7 wants to go to the free festival
8 does not sell any tickets

4 `1.68` Look at the Talk Builder. Listen and match the answers (a–f) with the questions (1–7)

a Saturday at eight o'clock.
b Of course (x 2).
c They cost from fifteen to thirty pounds.
d In the Southbank.
e Rock.
f There's a rap concert.

Talk Builder Asking for information

1 **Can we have some information about** concerts for this weekend, please? *b*
2 **What kind of** music do they play?
3 **How much** are the tickets?
4 **What other** concerts are there?
5 **Where** is the festival?
6 **What time** does it start?
7 **Can we have** two tickets, please?

⊙ SKILLS BUILDER 33

5 `1.69` Pronunciation Listen and repeat the questions.

6 Choose the best answer.

1 Can I have some information about concerts, please?
   a Good idea.   b Of course.   c No.
2 How much are the tickets?
   a Ten pounds.   b Of course.   c Sixty.
3 What time does it start?
   a In the afternoon.   b On Friday.
   c At nine o'clock.
4 Can I have two tickets, please?
   a No, you can't.   b Of course.   c I'm not sure.

7 ⊙ SKILLS BUILDER 32 **Read the strategies on page 113. Work in pairs. Check the information about the shows in Exercise 2.**

8 Work in pairs. Act out dialogues.

⊙ SKILLS BUILDER 33

1 **Choose three concerts for the weekend in your town/city. Write notes about:**
   • name of groups (international/local)
   • prices of tickets (from expensive to cheap)
   • day and time of concerts

2 **Practise saying expressions from the Talk Builder.**

3 **Work in pairs. Take turns to ask for information.**

A: *Can I have information about concerts for the weekend, please?*
B: *Sure. There's a Shakira concert on Friday.*
A: *How much are tickets?*

9 Tell the class about one of your partner's concerts.

There's a Shakira concert on Friday. Tickets cost a hundred euros.

Writing Workshop 2

① Read the emails (a–c). Match the sentences (1-5) with the people: Chloe, Georgina, Georgina and Chloe.

1 Wants to go out on Saturday. *Georgina and Chloe*
2 Wants to see the new film on Saturday.
3 Wants to go to a club.
4 Wants to meet at her house.
5 Her dad can collect them.

a Hi Chloe,
What are you up to at the weekend? Do you fancy going to the cinema on Saturday night? There's a new film with Emma Watson and Robert Pattinson. It starts at eight o'clock and tickets are £7. Why don't we meet at my place at seven?
Call me.
Georgina

b Hi there,
Thanks for the invitation. I want to see that film but I've got a better idea. There's a teen night at that new club (Igloo). Why don't we go? It starts at 9.00 on Saturday and tickets are £10. It's got live rap music (Dr Faustus) and a really good DJ!
Chloe

c Hi,
Okay, that's a great idea! Let's meet at my place at seven and my dad can take us there and collect us.
See you on Saturday!
G

Text Builder

② Match the expressions in blue from the notes with the meanings below (1-5).

1 At my house *at my place*
2 What are you doing … ?
3 Do you want to go … ?
4 Telephone me.
5 Thank you for …

③ Look at the Sentence Builder. How do you say the words in **bold** in your language?

Sentence Builder *and/but*

1 It starts at eight o'clock **and** tickets are £7.
2 I want to see that film **but** I've got a better idea.

→ SKILLS BUILDER 18

④ Complete the sentences with *and* or *but*.

1 That's a good suggestion __*but*__ I've got a better idea.
2 The film is good _____ it's got Keira Knightley and Brad Pitt in it - they're great!
3 It's a great café _____ the drinks are expensive.
4 I like that film _____ I don't like Emma Watson in it - she's not very good.
5 The tickets are expensive _____ the club is noisy.

⑤ Write a note to your partner inviting him/her to go out.

→ SKILLS BUILDER 19

1 **Choose one of the activities below (a-d). Write notes with information about it (time/ticket prices, etc.).**

   a a concert
   b a sports match (football/basketball)
   c a film or play
   d a teen night at a club

2 **Use your ideas to write a note to your partner.**

3 **Give your note to your partner. Write a reply to your partner's note with a new suggestion.**

⑥ Work in pairs. Read your partner's reply. Make more suggestions and agree on an activity for the weekend. Tell the class.

We want to go to a football match on Sunday afternoon. Tickets are €15 and it starts at five o'clock.

LEARNING LINKS: 1 Sound Choice 2 → MyLab / Workbook page 39. Choose three pronunciation activities to do.
2 Check Your Progress 3 → MyLab / Workbook page 40. Complete the **Module Diary.**

4 MEMORIES

Objectives: Listen, read, talk and write about memories; learn about the Past Simple.

TOPIC TALK

1 Work in pairs. Look at the dates in the network. Tell your partner the dates of the birthdays below.

My birthday is on the fifteenth of May.

- your birthday
- your parents' birthdays
- your best friend's birthday

2 2.1 **2.2** Listen to three descriptions of birthdays (1–3). Match them with the photos (a–c).

3 2.3 **2.4** Listen again to the first person. Complete the information in the network.

4 2.5 Pronunciation **Listen and write down the dates. Then listen again and repeat them.**

5 February 1999

LANGUAGE CHOICE 31: VOCABULARY PRACTICE

5 Work in pairs. Use the network to talk about *your* birthday memories.

Birthday memories

My birthday is on ¹ *22 July* .
My earliest birthday memory is my ²*fourth/fifth/sixth* birthday ³_____ .
My best birthday ever was ⁴_____ .
There was a ⁵*lunch at a restaurant/party on the beach/picnic in the country* with my ⁶*family/friends/girlfriend/boyfriend*.
The ⁷*food/music/dancing* was great!

Dates
the first of January, the second of February, the third of March, the fourth of April, the fifth of May, the sixth of June, the eleventh of July, the twelfth of August, the sixteenth of September, the twentieth of October, the twenty-second of November, the thirty-first of December

in 1999 (nineteen ninety-nine), 2004 (two thousand and four), 2007 (two thousand and seven), 2012 (twenty twelve)

- -

last month/August/year/summer, a year **ago**, two years **ago**

Warm Up

1 Look at the photos (a–b). Which teacher do you like? Use the words below to describe your favourite/least favourite teacher from primary school.

My favourite teacher was Miss Williams. She was strict but she was very friendly.

relaxed   young/old   attractive
friendly   serious   strict   funny

2 Read a school memory. Which words from Exercise 1 describe the teacher from the story?

3 Do similar things happen in your school? Do you have any funny school memories?

Past Simple

4 Complete the table with the past forms of the verbs below from the text.

~~have~~   ~~leave~~   come   go   ~~love~~   ~~show~~   tell
see   ask   laugh   talk   sit   answer   know

regular verbs (-*ed*)	*loved, showed*
irregular verbs	*had, left*

5 Read the sentences from the text and complete the rule.

1 *She **didn't talk** about boring things.*
2 *She **didn't give** us a lot of homework.*

- To make a negative sentence we put _____ in front of the infinitive.

6 Complete the sentences with the Past Simple forms of the verb *be*: *was/were* or *wasn't/weren't*.

	Affirmative	Negative
I/he/she/it	*Miss Sage* [1] *was young.*	*She* [3]_____ *very strict.*
we/you/they	*Her classes* [2]_____ *funny.*	*Her lessons* [4]_____ *boring.*

YOUR LETTERS   2.6

My history teacher, Miss Sage, was young and pretty. We loved her because she wasn't very strict and her lessons weren't boring. She didn't talk about boring things and she didn't give us a lot of homework – she showed us films and told us stories. She knew a lot of stories from history and her classes were often funny. She often sat on her desk and we just talked about the past.

One day in her lesson, a student from a different class came in. He saw Miss Sage on the desk and asked her: 'Hey, the head teacher wants to talk to Sage. Where is she?' Miss Sage wasn't angry, she answered: 'She went to the teachers' room'. The boy left the classroom and we all laughed. Miss Sage had a good sense of humour.

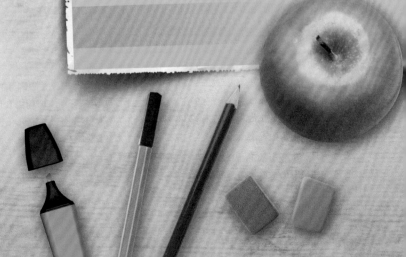

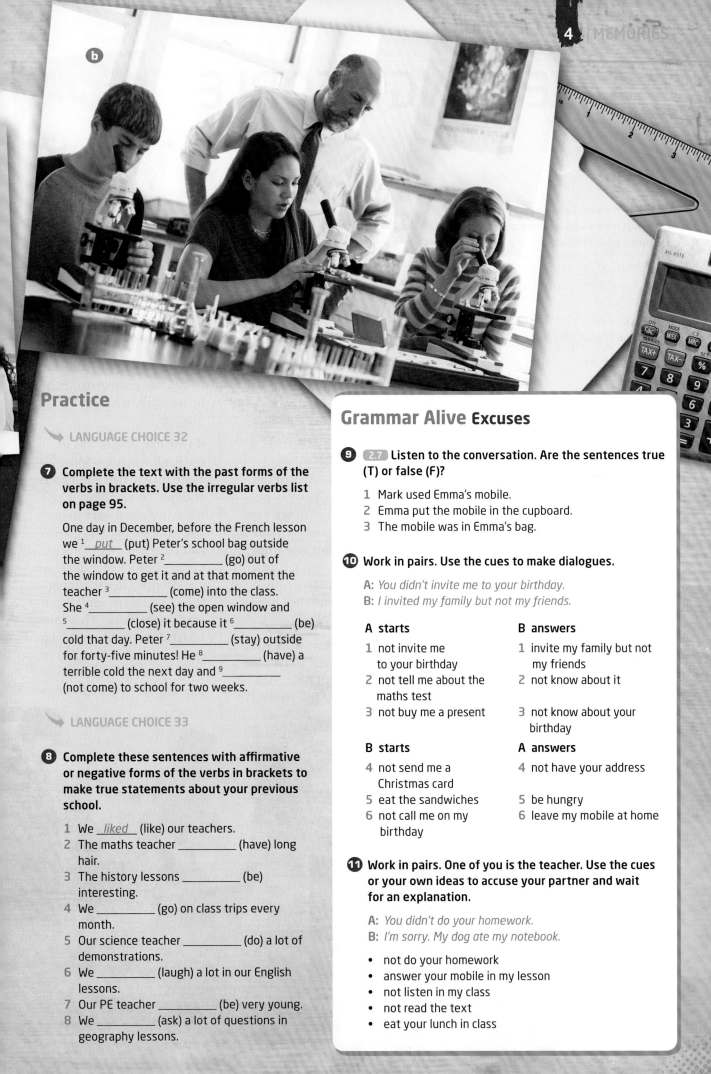

Practice

➤ LANGUAGE CHOICE 32

7 Complete the text with the past forms of the verbs in brackets. Use the irregular verbs list on page 95.

One day in December, before the French lesson we [1] _put_ (put) Peter's school bag outside the window. Peter [2]_____ (go) out of the window to get it and at that moment the teacher [3]_____ (come) into the class. She [4]_____ (see) the open window and [5]_____ (close) it because it [6]_____ (be) cold that day. Peter [7]_____ (stay) outside for forty-five minutes! He [8]_____ (have) a terrible cold the next day and [9]_____ (not come) to school for two weeks.

➤ LANGUAGE CHOICE 33

8 Complete these sentences with affirmative or negative forms of the verbs in brackets to make true statements about your previous school.

1 We _liked_ (like) our teachers.
2 The maths teacher _____ (have) long hair.
3 The history lessons _____ (be) interesting.
4 We _____ (go) on class trips every month.
5 Our science teacher _____ (do) a lot of demonstrations.
6 We _____ (laugh) a lot in our English lessons.
7 Our PE teacher _____ (be) very young.
8 We _____ (ask) a lot of questions in geography lessons.

Grammar Alive Excuses

9 **2.7** Listen to the conversation. Are the sentences true (T) or false (F)?

1 Mark used Emma's mobile.
2 Emma put the mobile in the cupboard.
3 The mobile was in Emma's bag.

10 Work in pairs. Use the cues to make dialogues.

A: *You didn't invite me to your birthday.*
B: *I invited my family but not my friends.*

A starts
1 not invite me to your birthday
2 not tell me about the maths test
3 not buy me a present

B answers
1 invite my family but not my friends
2 not know about it
3 not know about your birthday

B starts
4 not send me a Christmas card
5 eat the sandwiches
6 not call me on my birthday

A answers
4 not have your address
5 be hungry
6 leave my mobile at home

11 Work in pairs. One of you is the teacher. Use the cues or your own ideas to accuse your partner and wait for an explanation.

A: *You didn't do your homework.*
B: *I'm sorry. My dog ate my notebook.*

• not do your homework
• answer your mobile in my lesson
• not listen in my class
• not read the text
• eat your lunch in class

SKILLS
MEETING PEOPLE

Warm Up

1 Work in pairs. Tell your partner about when and where you met these people (a-c):

1 your partner in English class
   We met last year in the maths class.
2 your best friend
3 your English teacher

Reading

2 → SKILLS BUILDER 9 Use the strategies in the Skills Builder to match the headings (1-5) with the paragraphs (a-d) in the story. There is one extra heading.

1 Meeting again
2 War, studies and work
3 The army
4 Young love *a*
5 Family problems

3 Find four differences between the meeting in the story and the drawing opposite.

In the picture, Maggie has got a blue dress. In the story, she has got a red dress.

4 Read the story again. Are the sentences true (T) or false (F)?

1 Angus was in the army when he met Maggie. *F*
2 Maggie didn't want to see Angus when he came to her house.
3 Angus was angry with Maggie's parents.
4 After the war, Angus wanted to get married.
5 Angus saw Maggie first in the bank.
6 Maggie and Angus had a happy life.

FAMILY MEMORIES (2.8)

Readers send us stories and memories about their families.
Lucy Macdonald

a My granddad, Angus, was a teenager when World War II started. He was in love with a beautiful girl called Maggie. She was sixteen and he was seventeen but he wanted to go into the army. Before he left, Angus bought a ring and then went to Maggie's house.

b Maggie's parents opened the door and said, 'We're sorry but Maggie doesn't want to see you.' Angus was angry and went home but he did not know one thing; Maggie loved him but her parents did not like him because his family was poor and they lied to him.

c In the war, Angus was in Italy. In 1945, Angus went to London and finished his studies. Then he went to university and studied economics. He worked hard and did well in his exams. After he left university, Angus got a good job in a bank but he did not get married because he was still in love with Maggie.

d One day, Angus was in the bank when a woman came in. She had a red dress and hat – it was Maggie! He quickly walked over to her and said, 'Hello, Maggie, do you remember me?' Maggie nervously looked at him and dropped her shopping bag. There were apples and eggs on the floor! They got married that year and had four children. Sadly, they died in 2009 but they lived happily together for fifty-eight years.

5 Vocabulary Look at the Word Builder. Complete it with adverbs in blue in the text.

Word Builder Adverbs

Adjectives	Adverbs
Regular	**+ ly**
slow	slow**ly**
quick	1 _quickly_
nervous	2 _____
sad	3 _____
	+ ily
nois**y**	nois**ily**
happ**y**	4 _____
Irregular	
fast	fast
good	5 _____
hard	6 _____

LANGUAGE CHOICE 34:
VOCABULARY PRACTICE

6 Complete the sentences with the correct form of the words below.

hard ~~bad~~ angry fast sad good

1 I played _badly_ in the tennis game and I lost.
2 My brother can play the violin _____ . He is in the school orchestra.
3 _____ , my dog died last year.
4 My sister can run very _____ and often wins competitions.
5 My dad spoke to me _____ on Saturday night because I came home at twelve o'clock.
6 I worked very _____ and got an A in my Spanish exam.

Writing

7 Look at the Sentence Builder. How do you say the words in **bold** in your language?

Sentence Builder Time linkers

1 He was in the bank **when** a woman came in.
2 **Then** he went to university and studied economics.
3 Angus bought a ring **and then** went to Maggie's house.
4 **Before** he left, Angus bought a ring.
5 **After** he left university, Angus got a good job in a bank.

→ SKILLS BUILDER 20

LANGUAGE CHOICE 35

8 Choose the linkers below to complete the memory.

and then before then after when (x 2)

I was in the school library ¹ _when_ I met Alan. It was 25 June and I had a French exam the next day. It was about twelve o'clock ² _____ this tall guy came in. He sat down ³ _____ looked at me. He had a very nice smile. 'Can I use your dictionary?' he asked. ⁴ _____ we started to talk. We went to the cafeteria and had lunch. ⁵ _____ lunch, we went for a walk and he gave me his phone number. We met at the weekend and went to a club. ⁶ _____ I went out, I was very nervous. I put on my best dress. I was in love!

9 Write notes about meeting a person (real or invented).

1 **Where?** the tennis club in London
2 **When?** 8 May 2012
3 **His/Her appearance?** had long, dark hair and brown eyes
4 **What happened?** played a game - she won!
5 **Then?** then had a drink - met the next day and went to a club
6 **Then?** at the weekend came to my house for dinner - met my parents
7 **My feelings?** nervous/happy - was in love with her

10 Work in pairs. Tell your partner about your meeting.

I met Angela in the tennis club. It was 8 May and I ...

Your Choice

No Comment

'All you need is love.'

The Beatles, British pop group (1962–1970)

Warm Up

1 **Look at the photo. Is the man:**

a a burglar?
b a police officer?
c a guest?

2 **Read the interview about a burglary. Do you think Kate is a good witness?**

> (2.9)
>
> **Officer:** I phoned you last night about the burglary in your street. Can we talk now?
> **Kate:** Yes, of course.
> **Officer:** So when did it happen?
> **Kate:** It happened five days ago, at 9 p.m.
> **Officer:** Last Friday. Okay, where were you?
> **Kate:** I was in the kitchen with a friend.
> **Officer:** What did you see?
> **Kate:** It was dark but I saw a young woman in a green sports car. The woman was very slim, with long, blond hair.
> **Officer:** Was she worried or nervous?
> **Kate:** Yes, she was.
> **Officer:** Did you see the burglars?
> **Kate:** Yes, I did. I saw a tall, young man. He had a black bag. He got into the car and then they left very quickly.
> **Officer:** Did your friend see the man?
> **Kate:** No, she didn't. But she saw that woman yesterday in the shopping centre.

Past Simple: questions

3 **Complete the questions from the text in the table with *was/were* or *did*.**

	Questions	Short answers
be	¹ _Was_ she worried?	Yes, she **was**.
	Where ² _____ you?	
other verbs	³ _____ you see the burglars?	Yes, I **did**.
	⁴ _____ your friend see the man?	No, she **didn't**.
	What ⁵ _____ you see? When ⁶ _____ it happen?	

4 **Use the cues to ask Kate more questions.**

1 Where / you see the car?
   Where did you see the car?
2 How old / be the woman?
3 you / know the woman?
4 your friend / call the police?
5 What / the man do?
6 When / the man get in the car?

5 **Complete the police interview with Kate's friend. Make questions.**

1 _When did it happen_ ? It happened last weekend.
2 _____ ? I saw a green sports car and a woman.
3 _____ ? No, I didn't. I only saw the woman.
4 _____ ? She was in the car.
5 _____ ? Yes, she was. She was about twenty years old.

↘ LANGUAGE CHOICE 36

Grammar Alive Questioning

6 **(2.10) Listen to a witness. Complete the police officer's questions.**

1 Where _were you yesterday at 5 p.m._ ?
   → at the bus stop
2 Who _____ ? → a tall man
3 How old _____ ? → young
4 What colour _____ ? → black

7 **Work in pairs. Use the cues to ask and answer the questions about the robbery from Exercise 6.**

Where were you yesterday at 5 p.m.?
I was at the post office.

A answers	B answers
1 → at the post office	1 → in a shop
2 → a woman	2 → a boy
3 → about forty	3 → about sixteen
4 → green	4 → blue

Speaking Workshop 4

Angie

Zoe

Gary

1 Look at the photo. Match the girls (1–2) with the descriptions (a–c). There is one extra description.

1 Angie   a   Gary's sister
2 Zoe   b   Gary's girlfriend
          c   Zoe's friend

2 **2.11** **DVD 4** **Listen or watch** Listen to or watch the dialogue. Check your guesses from Exercise 1.

3 **2.11** **DVD 4** **Listen or watch** Listen to or watch the dialogue again. Answer these questions.

1 What does Zoe want to do?
2 What does Gary remember about his birthday?
3 Why is Gary not very happy when he meets Angie?
4 Why is Gary happy after he meets Angie?

4 **2.12** Look at the Talk Builder. Complete the sentences with these words. Then listen and check your answers.

> that (x 2)   after   then   because   ~~when~~   before

Talk Builder Talking about memories

A: **Do you remember** ¹ _when_ we went to that rock concert?
B: Oh, yes. **I remember** ² _____ .
A: **And** ³ _____ the concert, we had your birthday cake.
B: Yes, … and the concert was brilliant.
A: **Do you remember** the very tall girl?
B: **I don't remember** her name. She was a fantastic dancer.
A: **I don't remember** ⁴ _____ .
B: **You don't remember** ⁵ _____ you were with George all evening. **And** ⁶ _____ you went out for a pizza. **And** ⁷ _____ **that** you went home.

→ SKILLS BUILDER 34

5 **2.13** **Pronunciation** Listen and repeat sentences from the Talk Builder.

6 Work in pairs. Act out a dialogue about a memory.

→ SKILLS BUILDER 34

1 Choose a real memory or invent a memory about one of these things (a–d):

a   a party with your friends
b   a picnic in the country
c   a visit to a night club
d   a concert

2 Write notes to answer these questions below.

1 What was it?
2 When was it?
3 Who were you with?
4 What happened?
5 Was it funny/sad/exciting/boring?
6 What happened then?

3 → SKILLS BUILDER 35   Read the strategies. Do you do the same in your language?

4 Use your notes and the Talk Builder to act out a dialogue. Use the strategies from the Skills Builder to show interest.

A: *Do you remember when we went to that amusement park?*
B: *Yes, I remember that!*

7 Tell the class about your memory. Make guesses about your partners' memories – are they real or invented?

Language Review Modules 3 and 4

1 Going out/Memories **Complete the texts with the correct words.**

My town isn't big but there is a swimming ¹_____ and some art ²_____ . There is a good Italian ³_____ – I sometimes have pizza there. I don't go to our local ⁴_____ because it's very small and the films are old. I often go to the skate ⁵_____ in the town centre.
My birthday is ⁶*in/on* 1 August. We are on holiday in August so we usually have a picnic on the ⁷*country/beach*. My last birthday was different. We had dinner in a ⁸*dark/quiet* French restaurant. It was ⁹*expensive/comfortable* but the ¹⁰*food/music* was great. **/10**

2 Adverbs **Complete the text with the correct adverbs.**

11 My family work very _____ (hard) but at weekends we relax. We don't get up _____ (quick) or hurry all the time.
12 We eat our breakfast _____ (slow), talk a lot and cook together. My mum cooks really _____ (good) and she's our chef.
13 _____ (sad), the weekend is very short and it goes _____ (fast). **/6**

3 Verbs and prepositions/Time prepositions **Complete the sentences with *at, in, on* or *to*.**

14 I often go _____ the mountains _____ the autumn.
15 _____ Saturday mornings, I usually stay _____ home.
16 Listen _____ the radio programme _____ seven o'clock.
17 We live _____ South America but we go _____ London every year.
18 _____ the evening, we often go for a walk and look _____ the flowers in the park.
19 _____ Sundays, a lot of people go _____ the town centre and meet their friends. **/6**

4 Time linkers/*and, but* **Choose the correct words to complete the sentences.**

20 I was at school *when/but* the accident happened.
21 My parents went to school together *before/and* they got married.
22 I heard a noise and *when/then* a man broke the window.
23 *And/After* we had lunch, we went for a walk.
24 The food was great *then/but* the waiters were not very friendly.
25 I saw her *and/but* I fell in love. **/6**

5 Comparatives/Superlatives **Complete the sentences with the correct forms of the adjectives in brackets.**

Paris is ²⁶_____ (small) than London but it's ²⁷_____ (exciting) city in Europe.
I don't like Lady Gaga – she's ²⁸_____ (bad) pop singer in the world.
My house is ²⁹_____ (modern) than my friends' homes but it's ³⁰_____ (comfortable).
I'm not ³¹_____ (good) student in my class but I'm ³²_____ (good) at science than my friends. **/7**

6 Past Simple **Complete the dialogue with the verbs in the Past Simple tense.**

A: Hi Pete. What ³³_____ (you / do) last night?
B: I ³⁴_____ (stay) at home. And you?
A: I ³⁵_____ (go) to the cinema with Helen but she ³⁶_____ (not like) the film. It ³⁷_____ (be) a horror.
B: ³⁸_____ (she / leave) the cinema?
A: No, she didn't but she ³⁹_____ (not be) happy. **/7**

7 Asking for information **Choose the correct words to complete the questions.**

40 *Can I have/Do I have* some information, please?
41 *What time/Which* does it open?
42 *How much/How many* are the tickets?
43 Can I have a ticket, *please/thank you*? **/4**

8 Talking about memories **Put the phrases (a-d) in the correct places in the dialogue.**

a That wasn't funny.   c Do you remember
b We had a good time.   d And then

A: ⁴⁴_____ grandma's birthday last year?
B: Peter came with his new girlfriend, Sylvia.
A: ⁴⁵_____ he talked to Maggie all the time.
B: And Sylvia danced with me all the time. ⁴⁶_____
A: Peter got angry and left early.
B: ⁴⁷_____ Grandma wasn't happy. **/4**

Self Assessment

2.14 **Listen and check your answers. Write down your scores. Use the table to find practice exercises.**

Exercise	If you need practice, go to
1	Language Choice 25, 31
2	Language Choice 34
3	Language Choice 28, 29
4	Language Choice 35; SB p.38 ex.3
5	Language Choice 26, 27, 30
6	Language Choice 32, 33
7	SB p.37 ex.4
8	SB p.45 ex.4

LEARNING LINKS: **1** Read and listen to the story by Gerald Durrell in **Culture Choice 2** on page 99. Then do a project about a famous person from your country.
2 Exam Choice 2 → My Lab / Workbook pages 48-49.
3 Check Your Progress 4 → MyLab / Workbook page 50. Complete the **Module Diary.**

46

5 FITNESS

Objectives: Listen, read and **talk about** exercise and sport; **make** and **reply to** requests; **write** a note of invitation; **learn about** the Present Continuous.

TOPIC TALK

1 Find the activities in photos (a-c) in the network. Then match them with the descriptions below. Check your answers on page 116.

1 It started in 1875 in Canada and is very fast and dangerous.
2 It started in California in 1920 and is now an Olympic sport.
3 It started in India in about 2000 BC and is now popular in the West.

2 2.15 2.16 Listen to a conversation. Match Sue (S) and Nick (N) with these things (a-d):

a likes team sports S   c likes skateboarding
b doesn't like school sport   d is very fit

3 2.15 2.16 Listen again to the conversation. Complete the information in the network.

Exercise

I do sport ¹*once/twice/three/ four/five* times a week.
I don't like ² _____
but I like ³ _____ and I love ⁴ _____ .
I am ⁵*very/not very* fit.
I never ⁶ _____ .

Activities

climbing, cycling, dancing, horse riding, running, skateboarding, skiing, surfing, swimming, trekking
doing athletics, exercise, gymnastics, judo, yoga
playing basketball, beach volleyball, football, hockey, ice hockey, rugby, table tennis, tennis, volleyball

cycle/walk to school/the shops/my friends' houses, go to school by car, take the lift, walk up the stairs

4 2.17 Pronunciation Listen and repeat the words. Which letter can't you hear?

Climbing

➥ LANGUAGE CHOICE 37: VOCABULARY PRACTICE

5 Work in pairs. Use the network to talk about *your* exercise.

GRAMMAR
SUPER ATHLETES

Warm Up

1 Look at the photos (a-b). What are the sports? Do you know the athletes?

2 (2.18) Read and listen to the conversation. Why is Alan Oliveira an unusual athlete?

3 Do you think disabled athletes should take part in open competitions with other athletes? Why/Why not?

Present Continuous

4 Complete the sentences from the text with *am, is, are* or *am not*.

Affirmative
I ¹ _am_ **reading** a lot about disabled athletes.
She/He **is running**.
It ² _____ **starting** now.
We/You/They ³ _____ **doing** a project about Paralympics.

Negative
I ⁴ _____ **watching** football.
He **isn't running** very fast.
We/You/They **aren't reading**.

Questions	Short answers
⁵ _____ you **watching** football?	Yes, I **am**. / No, I**'m not**.
⁶ _____ he **wearing** artificial legs?	Yes, he **is**. / No, he **isn't**.
Are they **doing** a project?	Yes, they **are**. / No, they **aren't**.
What ⁷ _____ you **doing**?	

5 Read the sentences (1-4) from the text and match them with the uses (a-b).

1 *Look, it's starting!* a
2 *Now he is taking part in regular competitions.*
3 *I'm not watching football.*
4 *I'm reading a lot about disabled athletes.*

• We use the Present Continuous to talk about activities happening:
  a at the moment. b around now.

(2.18)

Mum: What are you doing, Pete? Are you watching football again?

Pete: No, I'm not watching football. It's a running competition – the men's 200 metres. Do you see that runner in the blue and green shirt? That's Alan Oliveira from Brazil. They call him 'the fastest man on no legs'.

Mum: Is he wearing artificial legs?

Pete: Yes, he is. Alan won a gold medal in the London Paralympics with them. And now he is taking part in regular competitions.

Mum: Amazing!

Pete: Yes, Alan can run really fast on those legs.

Mum: Look, it's starting now! Wow! He's good!

Pete: Yes, his legs are very high tech.

Mum: How do you know all this about him?

Pete: We are doing a project about the Paralympics at school so I'm reading a lot about disabled athletes.

a Alan Oliveira

b Natalia Partyka

Practice

6 Use the cues to write true sentences about this moment in the Present Continuous.

1 We / learn / English
  We're learning English.
2 I / run
3 My friends / play football
4 I / do an exercise
5 It / rain
6 The teacher / watch us
7 My best friend / sleep
8 We / listen to a song

7 Use the cues to write questions for 'around now' in the Present Continuous.

1 you / learn Spanish?
  Are you learning Spanish?
2 your class / watch English films this month?
3 you / prepare for an exam?
4 you / learn to drive?
5 your friends / do a lot of tests this week?
6 What / you / plan for your holidays?
7 We / work on a project this month?
8 I / work hard this week?

8 Work in pairs. Take turns to ask and answer the questions from Exercise 7.

A: *Are you learning Spanish?*
B: *No, I'm not.*

 LANGUAGE CHOICE 38

9 Complete the interview with a fan of Natalia Partyka, a Polish table tennis player.

Reporter: ¹ *Is she playing* (she / play) well?
Fan: Yes, I think she is really good today. She ² _____ (not win) at the moment but she ³ _____ (get) better.
Reporter: ⁴ _____ (you / have a good time) here in Sydney?
Fan: Yes, Natalia ⁵ _____ (play) very well in these championships. And this game is really exciting, we ⁶ _____ (enjoy) it a lot.

LANGUAGE CHOICE 39

Grammar Alive Describing a scene

10 **2.19** Listen to a telephone conversation. What are Julia, Polly, Martha and Chris doing?

Julia is relaxing.
Polly is …

11 Work in pairs. Use the cues to ask questions about Alan Oliveira and Natalia Partyka. Look at the photos to answer the questions.

A: *Is Alan cycling?*
B: *No, he isn't.*

A - ask about Alan Oliveira	B - ask about Natalia Partyka
1 cycle?	1 play table tennis?
2 drink water?	2 look at the ball?
3 talk?	3 move?
4 run?	4 smile?

12 Work in pairs. Look at the picture on page 119 for fifteen seconds. Then close your book. Take turns to ask and answer questions about what the people in the drawing are doing. Your partner corrects the mistakes.

A: *What is Mark doing?*
B: *He is walking the dog.*

SKILLS
GET FIT

Warm Up

1 How fit are you? Do you want to get fitter?

Reading

2 → SKILLS BUILDER 10 **Use the strategies to match the texts (1-3) with the list (a-c) below.**

a   a poster on a notice board
b   an online shopping website
c   an advert in a local paper

3 Read the texts again. Match the people (a-e) with the activities in the texts (1-3).

a   **Sally** likes night clubs. She doesn't like doing exercise but wants to lose weight. *2*
b   **Fred** runs marathons and is very fit but he wants to do a different activity.
c   **Jack** loves table tennis but hasn't got a table at home.
d   **Fiona** lives on the fifteenth floor and wants to get fit.
e   **Doug** wants to learn dancing and to get fit, too.

4 Look at the Sentence Builder. How do you say the words in **bold** in your language?

Sentence Builder *too/not enough*

1   A lot of exercise games are **too slow** or **not realistic enough**.
2   My living room is **not big enough** and I am **too tall**.

→ LANGUAGE CHOICE 40

1

KINECT SPORTS ⟨2.20⟩
by Microsoft
For Xbox 360
Price: £17.99
***** 57 customer reviews
The most useful review:
***** Mike G.
A lot of exercise games are too slow or not realistic enough but Kinect Sports is FANTASTIC! It's got volleyball, table tennis, football and athletics. It's not too difficult – my daughter is six and she can play the games. You can play against the computer, with family or friends or online. It's great fun. You move a lot and it's good exercise. My only problem is my living room – it's not big enough and I'm too tall!

2

ZUMBA WITH KAREN
Have fun and get fit!
Do you hate exercise but love dancing and parties? Well, Zumba is for you – it combines great Latin dancing with hard exercise (1000 calories an hour). I am an experienced Zumba trainer and there are usually twenty people in my classes.
Classes are only £5 an hour.
Karen Cooksey: kjcooksey@zmail.com
Tel: 05848 76628890
Ashford Health and Fitness Centre, 5 Cliff Road
Classes: 4 p.m. – 10 p.m., Monday to Friday

---

5 Complete the sentences with *too* or *not enough* and the adjectives in brackets.

1   I want to do ice hockey but my dad thinks it's
    too dangerous (dangerous).
2   I've got a new exercise game but it's _____ (fast) and it's boring.
3   We play football in my garden but it's _____ (big) - it's only twenty square metres.
4   Those dance classes are interesting but they're _____ (expensive) - they cost £10.
5   I want to do tower running but I'm _____ (fit) at the moment.
6   I think yoga is boring - it's _____ (slow) and you don't do a lot of exercise.

8 **Vocabulary** Look at the Word Builder. Match the multi-part verbs (1-5) with the meanings (a-e). How do you say them in your language?

a Please do it!
b What are you doing?
c Come to my house.
d I don't like …
e To leave home and go to the cinema, a café, etc.

> **Word Builder** Multi-part verbs (2)
>
> 1 What are you **up to**? *b*
> 2 Do you want to **go out**?
> 3 No, **I'm not into** skateboarding these days.
> 4 Oh, **come on**, Jamie! There's a great film on.
> 5 **Come round** here in twenty minutes.

➤ LANGUAGE CHOICE 41: VOCABULARY PRACTICE

9 Work in pairs. Take turns to act out the dialogue below. Change the words in *italics*.

A: What are you up to?
B: I'm *watching TV.*
A: Let's go out.
B: I don't know.
A: Let's *go swimming.*
B: I'm not really into *swimming.*
A: Oh, come on, Sue. A lot of our friends are at *the swimming pool.*
B: Okay, come round here in an hour.

10 Work in pairs. Choose five questions to ask your partner. Then suggest a new sport or type of exercise for him/her.

1 what / sport often do?
A: *What sport do you often do?*
B: *I play table tennis at home.*
2 usually walk to school/the shops/your friends' houses?
3 usually walk up the stairs or take the lift?
4 are you fit?
5 want to lose weight?
6 like hard exercise?
7 like dangerous sports/team sports/water sports?
8 how much time have you got?

Your Choice

5TH ALPHA TOWER RUN

WHEN
from 7.30 to 12.00 on 9 April 2012
WHERE
Alpha Tower, 12 Broad Street, Dinham
WHAT
run up 30 floors (93 metres) in under 15 minutes
WHO
fit people from 15 to 75 – it's very hard exercise!
REGISTRATION
£20 / £10 (students). The money goes to *Save the Children.*
CONTACT
Alice Barker, tel: 01585 8775234
FOR MORE INFORMATION
www.alphatowerrun.com

Listening

6 2.21 2.22 ➔ SKILLS BUILDER 3 Use the strategies to listen to three dialogues (1-3) and match them with the situations (a-d). There is one extra situation.

a a phone conversation between two friends *2*
b a phone conversation between a brother and sister
c a conversation at a party between two strangers
d a conversation between two students at school

7 2.21 2.22 Listen to the dialogues again. Are the sentences true (T) or false (F)?

1 Alan and Linda like athletics. *F*
2 They dance at the party.
3 Colin wants to go to the cinema.
4 Jamie and Colin meet at the cinema.
5 Alison is writing a letter.
6 They are late for the Zumba class.

> **No Comment**
>
> 'I buy those celebrity exercise videos. I love sitting and eating cookies and watching them.'
>
> *Dolly Parton*, American singer

15 GRAMMAR
A FITNESS FREAK

Warm Up

1 Do the questionnaire on page 116. Are you a fitness freak?

2 2.23 Read and listen to the conversation. Who is a fitness freak, Mark or Helen? Why?

Mark: Hi, Helen, do you want to go to the cinema on Friday night?

Helen: I can't. I'm playing tennis with my brother at seven o'clock.

Mark: What about Saturday? Are you doing anything on Saturday?

Helen: Yes, I'm going swimming in the afternoon and in the evening I'm doing a three-hour yoga session.

Mark: Wow! You *are* sporty! What about Sunday?

Helen: Well, in the morning, my dad is taking me to a horse-riding lesson. Then we're going running together. And in the afternoon I'm going to a Zumba class. You can come with me.

Mark: Er ... no. No, thanks.

Present Continuous: arrangements

3 Read the sentences (1–2) from the dialogue and choose the correct word in the rule. Find similar sentences in the text.

1 **I'm playing** tennis with my brother at seven o'clock.
2 In the morning, my dad **is taking** me to a horse-riding lesson.

- We use the Present Continuous tense to talk about *planned/unplanned* future activities.

4 Complete the dialogue with the correct form of the Present Continuous.

A: What ¹ _are you doing_ (you / do) at the weekend?
   ² _____ (you / go) away?
B: No, I'm not. My school ³ _____ (have) a swimming competition on Saturday. And you?
A: I ⁴ _____ (go) skiing with my dad.
B: When ⁵ _____ (you / come) home?
A: I'm back on Saturday evening – let's go to the cinema on Sunday.

5 Look at Mark's diary for next week. Write sentences about his arrangements. Is he into fitness and sport?

Mark is going to the cinema with Sue on Monday.

> **Monday**
> *go to the cinema with Sue*
> **Tuesday**
> *have dinner with Lily*
> **Wednesday**
> *meet Sandra*
> **Thursday**
> *have a Zumba class*
>
> **Friday**
> *meet friends at Tom's café*
> **Saturday**
> *go to see the Arsenal game*
> **Sunday**
> *go on a trip with Julia*

↘ LANGUAGE CHOICE 42

Grammar Alive
Talking about arrangements

6 2.24 Listen to the conversation. What are Nina's and Phillip's arrangements for the weekend?

Friday: *Nina's going to a basketball game.*

Saturday p.m. _____
Sunday a.m. _____
Sunday p.m. _____

7 Work in pairs. Use the cues to ask and answer questions about arrangements.

A: *What are you doing tonight?*
B: *I'm going to a concert.*

A starts	B answers
1 tonight	1 go to a concert
2 on Friday afternoon	2 do a yoga class
3 on Saturday morning	3 have a driving lesson
B starts	**A answers**
4 after school	4 go to the dentist
5 on Saturday	5 meet a friend
6 on Sunday	6 have lunch with my family

8 Work in pairs. Ask and answer about your arrangements for the weekend.

A: *What are you doing on Saturday?*
B: *I'm going to the theatre.*

Speaking Workshop 5

1 Look at the photos. What are they doing?

2 2.25 DVD 5 Listen or watch Listen to or watch the dialogue. Check your guess from Exercise 1. Are the sentences true (T) or false (F)?

1 Patsy hasn't got any tennis things when she arrives. *T*
2 Patsy uses a pair of Zoe's trainers.
3 They play tennis in the garden.
4 Zoe plays very well.
5 Zoe wants to continue but Patsy is tired.
6 Patsy likes 'virtual tennis'.

3 Look at the Talk Builder. How do you say the words in **bold** in your language?

> **Talk Builder** Requests and replies
>
> | | Agree | Refuse |
> |---|---|---|
> | 1 **Can you lend me** some shorts, please? | **Sure, no problem.** | **Sorry**, I can't because ... |
> | 2 **Could we play again** next Saturday? | **Okay.** **No problem.** | |
>
> ⊝ SKILLS BUILDER 36

4 2.26 Pronunciation Listen and repeat the requests.

5 Match the requests (1-5) with the reasons (a-e).

1 Can you lend me your dictionary, please? *c*
2 Could you help me with my homework, please?
3 Can you give me a glass of water, please?
4 Can you lend me a hat, please?
5 Can you lend me your mobile, please?

a Mine isn't working.
b It's very cold.
c I left mine at home.
d I'm very thirsty.
e I don't understand this question.

6 Speaking Work in pairs. Ask and answer the questions from Exercise 5. Use expressions from the Talk Builder to reply.

7 Work in pairs. Act out one of the role-plays.

⊝ SKILLS BUILDER 36

1 **Choose one of the situations (a-d).**
   a you are at a sports centre with a friend
   b you are on holiday with a friend
   c you are in class with your partner
   d you are at home with your brother/sister

2 **Think of requests to make to your partner and reasons for your requests.**
   b *borrow his/her camera (haven't got a camera) / give me some water (am thirsty)*

3 **Work in pairs. Act out your situations. Take turns to ask requests.**
   A: *Hey, Monika. Can you lend me your camera, please? I haven't got a camera.*
   B: *I'm sorry, I can't because ...*

8 Which requests did your partner agree to? Tell the class.

Monika lent me her mobile phone.

Writing Workshop 3

1 **Read the notes (a–c). Are the sentences true (T) or false (F)?**

1 Tom, Lucy and Oliver like playing volleyball. *T*
2 Lucy can't come because it's her birthday.
3 Oliver wants to come to the game with a friend.
4 Oliver can't come to the cinema because he's shopping.

a Hi there,

I'm organising a volleyball game at the local sports centre at 11.00 on Saturday morning. Then we're having lunch in the sports centre café. There's a new Matt Damon film so we're going to the cinema after lunch.
Would you like to come?
Please, send me a text or call me.
See you,
Tom

b Hi there Tom,

Thanks for the invitation. I'd like to come but I can't because I'm busy on Saturday. It's my cousin's birthday so she's having a party. Another time maybe — I love playing volleyball!
Thanks anyway,
Lucy

c Hi Tom,

Thanks for your invitation. I'd love to come to the game! Can I bring my friend, Harry? He's a good player. I'm sorry but I can't come to the cinema because I'm going to a football match with my dad.
See you on Saturday.
Cheers,
Oliver

Text Builder

2 **Read the texts again. Which of the expressions in blue:**

1 say hello to people?
   Hi / Hi there
2 finish the notes?
3 ask for a reply?
4 invite people to come?
5 refuse an invitation?
6 accept an invitation?

3 **Look at the linkers in the Sentence Builder. Look at the other examples of *so* and *because* in the text. How do you say the linkers in your language?**

> **Sentence Builder** Linkers *because* and *so*
>
> 1 There's a new Matt Damon film **so** we're going to the cinema.
> 2 We're going to the cinema **because** there's a new Matt Damon film.
>
> → SKILLS BUILDER 21

4 **Use the words in brackets to rewrite the sentences. Start with the underlined words.**

1 I can't come because <u>I'm busy</u>. (so)
   I'm busy so I can't come.
2 I'm going shopping so <u>I can't</u> come. (because)
3 I'm having a party because <u>it's my</u> birthday. (so)
4 There's a concert so <u>we're going to</u> that club. (because)
5 I'm going to dance classes because <u>I want to</u> be fit. (so)

5 **Write a note of invitation to a friend.**

→ SKILLS BUILDER 22

1 **Choose one of the activities (a–c).**

   a a sporting event (e.g. a football game/a tennis competition)
   b a party (at home/in a café)
   c a night out (a film/dinner at a café/dancing at a club)

2 **Write notes about these things:**

   • the place   • the day and time
   • the activities

3 **Use your notes to write an invitation.**

6 **Give your invitation to your partner and he/she replies to it.**

**LEARNING LINKS: 1 Sound Choice 3 → MyLab / Workbook page 59. Choose three pronunciation activities to do.
2 Check Your Progress 5 → MyLab / Workbook page 60. Complete the Module Diary.**

MODULE 6 AGE

Objectives: Listen, **read** and **talk about** people; **describe** people in photos; **write** sentences to describe people; **learn more** about present tenses and questions.

a My granddad
b My neighbour
c My brother
d My cousin

TOPIC TALK

1 **Look at the photos (a–d) and the network. Make guesses about the people.**

The man in photo a is about seventy. He is a gardener. He is probably friendly.

2 2.27 2.28 **Listen to Lucy's descriptions of her family (a–d). Check your guesses from Exercise 1.**

3 2.29 2.30 **Listen again to the first description. Complete the information in the network.**

4 2.31 **Pronunciation Listen and repeat words from the network. Notice the sound of the last syllable.**

bus driver student

> LANGUAGE CHOICE 43: VOCABULARY PRACTICE

5 **Work in pairs. Use the network to tell your partner about your family members or friends.**

People

Eric is a ¹ _pensioner_ .
He is ² _____ years/months old.
He *is/was* a ³ _____ .
He is interested in
⁴*music/gardening/reading/sport.*
He is very ⁵ _____ and ⁶ _____ .

baby, child, teenager, pensioner

Age
six months, eleven months, eighteen months, nine, nineteen, twenty-one, sixty-three, seventy-nine, about fifteen, about thirty-five, about fifty, about sixty

Occupations
bus driver, doctor, engineer, gardener, lawyer, nurse, office worker, police officer, shop assistant, primary school/secondary school/ university student, teacher, vet, waiter/waitress

Personality
clever, friendly, hard-working, kind, moody, outgoing, shy, talkative, tidy

55

16 GRAMMAR
TEENAGE BRAINS

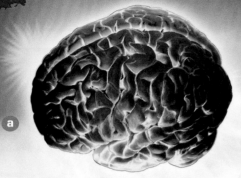

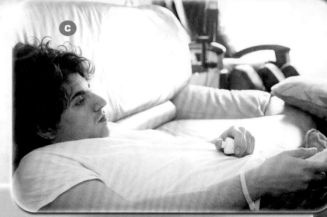

Warm Up

1 Look at photo (a) of the human brain and answer the questions. Check your answers on page 117.

1 The adult brain weighs about:
   a 900g.   b 1600g.   c 1350g.
2 The brain has _____ of neurons and brain connections.
   a thousands   b millions   c billions
3 The brain uses _____ of our body's energy.
   a 20%   b 5%   c 15%

2 Look at the photos (b–c). Which of these things are true about teenagers?

- They often feel tired in the morning.
- They are not usually very good planners.
- They often can't control their emotions.

3 Read the text to check your guesses.

4 Are you a 'typical' teenager? Which of the things from the text do you do?

Present Simple and Continuous

5 Complete the table with the names of the tenses, Present Simple or Present Continuous. Find more examples of the two tenses in the text.

1_____	2_____
Two people **are sleeping**. Your biological rhythm **is changing**.	Teens **sleep** longer at weekends. Our brain **needs** sleep every day.

6 Match the tenses in Exercise 5 (Present Simple and Present Continuous) with the uses (a–b).

a things happening right now or around now
b things happening regularly or always true

Science today Q&A   2.32

Q It's the first lesson today and I can't concentrate. Two people are sleeping! What is the problem?

A It's normal, your biological rhythm is changing – you wake up later and go to bed later.
Also, teenagers need 9.5 hours of sleep. When they sleep less than six hours, they can't concentrate and become moody. Some teens sleep longer at weekends but the brain needs sleep to 'work on' new information.

Q My teenage brother has got an exam tomorrow and he's going out to a party. Is this normal?

A Your brother is a teenager. His brain is still developing. He probably doesn't plan things or think of the consequences of his actions. The 'planning' part of our brains develops less quickly and a lot of teenagers can't organise their time well or control their emotions.

Q My sister watches TV all day. She is watching a silly programme right now. Is this healthy?

A The teenage brain has billions of neurons and brain connections. When teenagers do a lot of things like science or sport, their brain develops the connections for these activities. When they watch a lot of TV, the brain doesn't use these connections and loses them. So a lot of TV isn't great for teenagers.

Practice

7 Which sentence (a or b) can people (1-4) say?

1 a student in front of the TV
   a I'm studying hard. (b)I study hard.
2 a teenager in a lesson
   a I'm not sleeping.   b I don't sleep.
3 a teacher at a restaurant
   a I teach English. b I'm teaching English.
4 a girl in a library
   a I'm looking for information about China.
   b I look for information about China.

➤ LANGUAGE CHOICE 44

8 Complete the interview with a teenager with the verbs in brackets in the Present Simple or Present Continuous.

A: How long ¹_do you sleep_ (you / sleep) every night?
B: I ²_____ (not go) to bed before 10 p.m. and I
   ³_____ (get) up at 6.30 a.m. But this is different because we've got exams. I ⁴_____ (revise) until midnight.
A: But you ⁵_____ (not / study) now. What ⁶_____ (you / do)?
B: I ⁷_____ (wait) for my English exam. I'm really nervous.
A: What ⁸_____ (you / drink)? Is this coffee?
B: No, I ⁹_____ (not like) coffee. I ¹⁰_____ (drink) water to keep my brain active. It's healthier than coffee.

9 Look at the drawings (a-d) and use the cues (1-4) to write two sentences about each drawing: one in the Present Simple and one in the Present Continuous.

1 teach English / talk to a student
   He teaches English. He's talking to a student.

2 go to school / play football
3 work in a hospital / write an email
4 study languages / drink tea

➤ LANGUAGE CHOICE 45

Grammar Alive
Talking about activities

10 🔊 **2.33** Listen to the conversation. What do Mary and Jim usually read? What are they reading now? Why?

Mary usually reads fashion magazines but now …

11 Work in pairs. Use the cues to ask and answer the questions.

A: *Do you always sleep on the sofa?*
B: *No, I don't. I'm sleeping on the sofa this week because my cousins are sleeping in my room.*

A starts	B answers
1 always sleep on the sofa?	1 this week / my cousins – sleep in my room
2 usually use a laptop?	2 use a laptop today / my brother – use my computer
3 often read newspapers?	3 read a newspaper now / look for some news

B starts	A answers
4 often watch football on TV?	4 watch this match / Ronaldo – play
5 often cook meals at your home?	5 cook lunch today / my parents – work
6 always go to school by bus?	6 this week / the underground – not work

12 Use the time expressions below to write sentences about what you, your family and friends do and are doing.

My sister usually goes out in the afternoon. This month she's preparing for her driving test.

- this week/month
- right now
- today
- often
- usually
- at weekends

17 SKILLS
MY RIGHTS

Warm Up

1 Match the photos (a–c) with three things in the list.

1 drive a car
2 leave school and get a job
3 get the same pay as an adult
4 go into the army
5 get married
6 vote in national and local elections
7 smoke cigarettes

2 **Your Culture** Work in pairs. At what age can young people in your country legally do the things in Exercise 1?

1 *You can drive a car when you are eighteen.*

Reading

3 Read the magazine article. When can young people in Britain do the things in Exercise 1?

1 *You can drive a car when you are seventeen.*

4 ➡ SKILLS BUILDER 11 Use the strategies to choose the best answers to the questions.

1 Why are the two young people angry?
  a because they can't vote in elections
  b because teenagers haven't got any rights
  c because they can't drive
  d because teenagers can't do a lot of things

2 When do British young people get 'adult pay'?
  a when they are sixteen
  b when they are twenty-one
  c when they are eighteen
  d when they are twenty

3 How does Rajiv get the same pay for young people in his area?
  a he talks to local teenagers
  b he is in the UK Youth Parliament
  c he writes to magazines
  d he talks to local business people

4 Who does Alice want the vote for?
  a sixteen, seventeen and eighteen-year-olds
  b fifteen and sixteen-year-olds
  c sixteen and seventeen-year-olds
  d seventeen and eighteen-year-olds

5 What does Alice want?
  a more traffic and cars
  b more bicycles and people
  c more space for cars and bicycles
  d more space for people and bicycles

Teen POLITICS (2.34)

Teen Campaigners

In Britain, when you are sixteen you can leave school and work but you don't get the same pay as adults. When you are seventeen you can drive a car but you can't vote. Two young campaigners are angry about this and wrote to our magazine.

SAME JOB, SAME PAY

Rajiv Gupta is a student at Nower Hill School in London. He was a representative in the UK Youth Parliament when he was fourteen. Rajiv's campaign is about teenage pay. Teenage workers only get sixty percent of adult pay when they are sixteen or seventeen and eighty percent when they are eighteen, nineteen or twenty. 'We do the same jobs – why can't we have the same pay?' he asks. Rajiv visits shops and offices and talks about teenage pay. He is quite happy about his campaign – some local businesses now pay teenagers the same as adults because of his visits!

WHERE'S OUR VOTE?

Alice Coates is a teenager from Bristol with an outgoing personality. She is a student in Year 10, is studying politics at school and wants to be a lawyer. Alice's campaign is to get votes for people when they are sixteen and seventeen. 'When you are sixteen,' she says, 'you can smoke, get married and go into the army – but you can't vote. It's really unfair!' A lot of young people are not very interested in politics but Alice's campaign is very popular with Britain's 1.7 million sixteen and seventeen-year-olds. What does Alice want to vote for? 'I want less traffic and more space for people and bicycles!'

5 Vocabulary Look at the Word Builder. How do you say the words in **bold** in your language?

> **Word Builder** Modifiers
>
> 1 They are **not very** interested in politics.
> 2 He is **quite** happy about his campaign.
> 3 Her campaign is **very** popular.
> 4 It's **really** unfair!

↘ LANGUAGE CHOICE 46: VOCABULARY PRACTICE

6 Use the cues to write sentences about *you*.

I am very interested in politics.

- interested in politics/music/sport
- outgoing/tidy/hardworking

Writing

7 Look at the Sentence Builder. Translate the sentences into your language.

> **Sentence Builder** Information about people
>
> 1 Alice is a teenager **from** Bristol.
> 2 She is a person **with** an outgoing personality.
> 3 She is a student **in** Year 10.
> 4 Rajiv is a student **at** Nower Hill School.
> 5 He was a representative **in** the UK Youth Parliament
>
> ➔ SKILLS BUILDER 23

8 Use the cues and the Sentence Builder to make sentences.

1 my brother / student / Cambridge University
   My brother is a student at Cambridge University.
2 my sister / student / Year 7
3 she / person / friendly personality
4 my mum / teacher / a primary school
5 my cousin / teenager / Scotland
6 he / athlete / a lot of medals

↘ LANGUAGE CHOICE 47

9 Write five sentences about the people in *your* family.

My brother is a player in the school football team.

10 Choose a person at your school. Use expressions from the Word and Sentence Builders to write sentences about him/her.

She is a student in Year 10. She is really interested in hockey and she is a player in the school team.

11 Work in pairs. Read your partner's sentences. Ask questions and try to guess who it is.

A: *Is it a person in this class?*
B: *No, it isn't.*

No Comment

'Get up, stand up. Stand up for your rights!'

Bob Marley, Reggae artist

Your Choice

18 AGE QUIZ

Warm Up

1 Do the quiz about age. Check your answers on page 117.

1 **How old was the oldest person in history?**
a 115   b 122   c 119
2 **Who lives longer – men or women?**
a men   b women
3 **How long did people live in ancient Rome?**
a 33 years   b 44 years
c 28 years
4 **Where in the world do people live the longest?**
a Spain   b Japan   c the USA
5 **What lives longer than people?**
a gorillas   b elephants   c trees
6 **When do people usually start going grey?**
a about 50   b about 30   c about 70
7 **Why do babies sleep a lot?**
a they are tired   b their bodies are changing
c their eyes need rest
8 **Which part of their memory do old people lose first?**
a general knowledge   b memories of the past
c remembering new things

Questions

2 Look again at the quiz and answer the questions (1-3).

1 What question words ask about *people, things, place, time* and *reason*?
2 What question words ask about *age* and *length*?
3 Complete these questions about *size, height* and *distance*:
_____ big is it? _____ tall is he?
_____ far is it?

3 Complete the questions with *who, what, where, when, which, why* or *how.*

1 _How_ long do women live in Japan?
2 _____ are the signs of aging?
3 _____ does the oldest living person live?
4 _____ invented old people's homes?
5 _____ do old people sleep less than young people?
6 _____ part of our brain develops slowest?
7 _____ do young people need the most sleep?

↘ LANGUAGE CHOICE 48

4 Read the interview with a memory expert (E). Complete the questions in the Sentence Builder.

E: We studied the brains and memory of teenagers and adults.
Q: **Who did you examine?**
E: Fifty adults aged twenty-five to thirty-five.
Q: **So who examined the teenagers?**
E: My two assistants. They examined seventy boys and girls.

Sentence Builder
Questions about subject/object

Question about the **subject**:
Who _____ the teenagers?
→ My assistants.

Question about the **object**:
Who _____ you _____ ?
→ Fifty adults.

5 Write questions about the missing information in the sentences.

1 ... live over 100 years. Who _____?
Who lives over 100 years?
2 We are examining ... Who _____?
3 I like comedy films. ... What films _____?
4 ... have grey hair. Who_____?
5 They like ... What _____?

Grammar Alive
Sharing personal information

6 **2.35** Listen to the interview. How different is your life from Janet's? Write three differences.

I don't live with my grandparents. I finish school at 5 p.m.

7 **2.35** Listen to the interview again and complete the questions (a-h). Then work in pairs and ask and answer the questions.

a How old _are you_ ?
b _____ is your family?
c _____ does the housework in your home?
d _____ cooks in your home?
e _____ finish school?
f _____ in your free time?
g _____ go out?
h Where _____ ?

Speaking Workshop 6

1 **Vocabulary** Look at the vocabulary box below. Describe the clothes of the people (1-5) in the photo.

2 *That girl is wearing blue jeans and a brown top.*

Clothes
coat, dress, hat, jacket, jeans, jumper, shirt, shorts, skirt, top, trousers, T-shirt

2 **2.36** **DVD 6** **Listen or watch** Listen to or watch the dialogue. Choose the best answer to these questions.

1 Where did Steve and Bob go?
   a to a party   b to a club   c to the cinema
2 Who is Matt's girlfriend?
   a Isabel   b Sandra   c Debbie
3 Who is Matt's best friend?
   a Sam   b Dave   c Mark
4 Which girl does Steve like?
   a Sandra   b Debbie   c Isabel

3 **2.36** **DVD 6** **Listen or watch** Listen to or watch the dialogue again. Match the names with the people in the picture (1-5).

Mark, Sandra, Sam, Isabel, ~~Matt~~

Matt – 3

4 Look at the Talk Builder. How do you say the words in **bold** in your language?

Talk Builder Describing people in photos

A: This is the best ¹one. It's a photo of my cousin, Matt, and his friends.
B: Which ²one's your cousin?
A: Matt's the guy **on the left** in the green jumper. He's standing **at the front**.
B: Which of the girls is his girlfriend?
A: She's standing **next to** him. She's the ³one in the jeans and the brown top.
B: Who are those guys **at the back**?
A: The ⁴one **in the middle** with the blonde hair is Matt's best friend.
B: And who's that guy in the orange shirt **on the right**? Sam?

➔ SKILLS BUILDER 37

5 Look at the Talk Builder again. Which of the things below (a-d) does **one** refer to in the examples (1-4)?

a guy *4*   c person
b girl   d photo

6 Complete the sentences.

A: This is a photo of my family.
B: Which ¹_one_ is your mum?
A: She's the person in the ²_____ of the group. She's sitting ³_____ to my dad.
B: ⁴_____ of the children is your sister?
A: She's the ⁵_____ with red hair.

7 Work in groups and talk about a photo.

➔ SKILLS BUILDER 37

1 **Choose a photo of your friends or family. Bring it to class.**

2 **Write notes about these things:**
   • their names
   • information about them (age/occupation/personality)
   • what they are wearing
   • where they are in the photo

3 ➔ SKILLS BUILDER 38 **Work in groups. Use the hesitation strategies to help you answer questions about your photos.**

A: *Who is the woman in the middle in the red dress?*
B: *Er … that's my aunt Julia. She's a teacher, you know.*

8 Which of the photos of the group is the most interesting? Tell the class.

Anna's photo of her friends at an amusement park is the most interesting.

Language Review Modules 5 and 6

1 Exercise/People/Clothes **Complete the text with the correct words.**

My cousin Barbara is quite fit. She goes swimming three [1]_____ a week and she [2]_____ yoga every day. She always [3]_____ up the stairs and never [4]_____ the lift. On Sundays, she [5]_____ table tennis with her friends. Barbara is seventeen. She is a [6]*pensioner/teenager* but she would like to be a police [7]*officer/student*. In the summer, she works as a shop [8]*worker/assistant* in a clothes shop for men. She sells trousers, [9]*skirts/shirts* and jumpers. People like her because she is [10]*moody/kind* and friendly. **/10**

2 Multi-part verbs (2) **Complete the dialogue with** *into, on, out, round* **or** *up.*

A: Hi, Carla. It's Jeff. What are you [11]_____ to?
B: I'm reading.
A: Let's go [12]_____ . There's a free jazz concert in the park.
B: I'm not [13]_____ jazz. I want to finish my book.
A: Oh, come [14]_____ , Carla. Concerts are always fun!
B: Okay then, I can finish it tomorrow. Come [15]_____ in half an hour. **/5**

3 *too, enough/because, so* **Rewrite the sentences using the new beginnings and the words in brackets.**

16 I'm interested in football so I'm watching this game. (because)
I'm watching this game _____ .
17 I invited him because he's very nice. (so)
He's very nice _____ .
18 Our house is too small. (enough)
Our house is _____ .
19 Arsenal are not fast enough today. (too)
Arsenal are _____ . **/4**

4 Present Continuous **Complete the dialogue with the verbs in brackets.**

A: [20]_____ (you / work) Steve?
B: I [21]_____ (try) to write a letter. Why?
A: I [22]_____ (do) my Spanish homework and I've got some problems. And we [23]_____ (have) a test tomorrow.
B: Ask Mary! She [24]_____ (study) Spanish this year and she [25]_____ (not do) any important things at the moment. And I haven't got a lot of time. I [26]_____ (go out) at six o'clock.
A: Have you got a date? [27]_____ (you / meet) a new girl?
B: I [28]_____ (not meet) a girl. I [29]_____ (play) football with some friends tonight. **/10**

5 Present Simple and Continuous **Complete the sentences with the verbs in brackets in the correct tense.**

My parents are scientists. They [30]_____ (work) at university. This year, they [31]_____ (study) brains. This film is really boring! Look! Mia [32]_____ (sleep). She [33]_____ (not like) love stories.
I normally [34]_____ (go out) in the evening but this week I [35]_____ (work) on my science project. **/6**

6 Questions **Ask questions about the underlined information.**

36 <u>Julia</u> is crying because her dog got lost.
37 <u>My mother</u> cooked lunch.
38 I bought <u>music magazines</u>.
39 My sister loves <u>Harry Potter</u>.
40 I got up <u>at six o'clock</u>.
41 My brother is <u>1.86 m tall</u>. **/6**

7 Requests and replies **Match the requests (42-44) with the replies (a-c).**

42 Can you close the window?
43 Can you lend me your laptop?
44 Can you wait a minute?
a Okay, I'm cold, too.
b Sure, I've got a lot of time.
c Sorry, but I left it at home. **/3**

8 Describing photos/information about people **Complete the dialogue with the correct words.**

A: This is a photo of my family. I'm here [45]_____ the right.
B: Who is the girl [46]_____ black hair?
A: The [47]_____ on the left? It's Alicia, my cousin [48]_____ Liverpool.
B: Which one is your mother?
A: She's the woman [49]_____ the middle in a green dress. And my father is [50]_____ the back. **/6**

Self Assessment

`2.37` Listen and check your answers. Write down your scores. Use the table to find practice exercises.

Exercise	If you need practice, go to
1	Language Choice 37, 43
2	Language Choice 41
3	Language Choice 40; SB p.54 ex. 3
4	Language Choice 38, 39
5	Language Choice 44, 45
6	Language Choice 48
7	SB p.53 ex.3
8	SB p.61 ex.4

LEARNING LINKS: 1 Read and listen to the story by Lewis Carroll in **Culture Choice 3** on page 103. Then do a project about a character from your country's literature.
2 Exam Choice 3 → My Lab / Workbook pages 68-69.
3 Check Your Progress 6 → MyLab / Workbook page 70. Complete the **Module Diary.**

7 CINEMA

Objectives: Listen, read and talk about films; write a formal email asking for information; learn about *going to* for the future and *have to/don't have to.*

TOPIC TALK

1 Look at the photos (a–c) and the network. What types of films are they?

2 `2.38` `2.39` Listen to three people talking about films. Check your answers from Exercise 1. Which of the people (1–3) like these things?

- action films
- great dialogues
- romantic comedies
- Johnny Depp
- westerns
- Reese Witherspoon

3 `2.40` `2.41` Listen again to the first person. Complete the information in the network.

My films

My favourite types of films are ¹*animations* and ²_____ but I don't like ³_____ . My favourite ⁴_____ is Johnny Depp. My favourite film is *Toy Story 3* because it's got great ⁵_____ and ⁶_____ ⁷*animation.*

→ LANGUAGE CHOICE 49:
VOCABULARY PRACTICE

4 `2.42` Pronunciation Listen to three sentences and write down the words. Listen again and underline the unstressed words.

1 *She is a brilliant actress.*

5 Work in pairs. Use the network to talk about *your* favourite films.

A: *What films do you like?*
B: *I like thrillers and dramas. And you?*

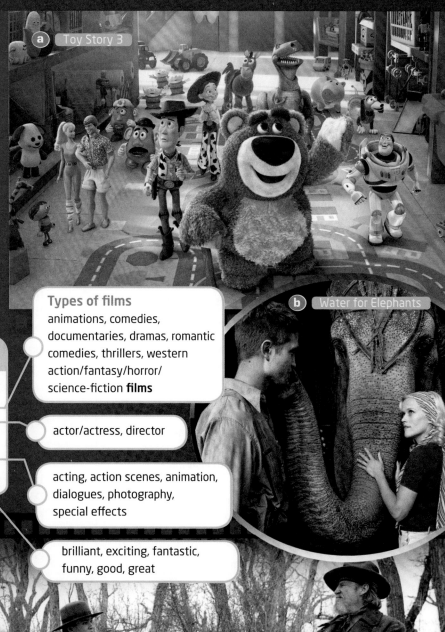

a Toy Story 3

b Water for Elephants

c True Grit

Types of films
animations, comedies, documentaries, dramas, romantic comedies, thrillers, western action/fantasy/horror/ science-fiction **films**

actor/actress, director

acting, action scenes, animation, dialogues, photography, special effects

brilliant, exciting, fantastic, funny, good, great

TICKET

63

GRAMMAR
FILM MAKERS

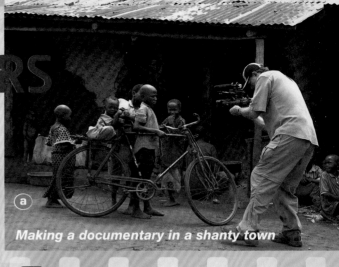

(a)

Making a documentary in a shanty town

Warm Up

1 Look at the photos (a–b). Do you think these documentaries are interesting? Why/Why not?

2 Read an interview with a young film maker. What films does she:

a make?
b watch online?
c want to make?

3 Do you or your friends make short films? Do you put them online? Do you watch other people's films online? What kind of films do you watch?

Future: *be going to*

4 Complete the sentences from the text. What time do they talk about: past, present or future?

Affirmative
I [1] *am* **going to visit** India next year. She/He **is going to film** the poor areas of the town. We/You/They [2] _____ **going to show** our best films.

Negative
I' [3] _____ **not going to be** a film maker. He/She **is not going to shoot** documentaries. We/You/They **are not going to visit** India.

Questions	Short answers
[4] _____ **you going to study** at a film school? **Is** he/she **going to film** people in our town? What **are** you **going to film**?	Yes, I **am**. / No, I'**m not**. Yes, he/she **is**. / No, he/she **isn't**.

5 Which sentence (a or b) means the same as the sentence below?

I'm going to make films.

a I'm planning to make films.
b I'm making films.

6 Look at these time expressions from the text. Translate them into your language.

- in four months' time
- next year
- this year

(2.43)

A lot of amateur film makers put their original films online. We talk to Paula Harmon from New York.

Interviewer: What films do you make, Paula?
PH: My friends and I film unicyclists here in New York. They do amazing things! We put our videos online and we watch amateur videos so we can learn things from them. We're going to show our best films at a special unicyclists' meeting in four months' time.

I: Do you watch videos online?
PH: Yes, I do. A lot of people put fantastic things online! Now I'm looking for travel documentaries from India because I'm going to visit the country next year.

I: Why do people upload their films?
PH: They want to share them. I've got a friend in Kenya. He films everyday life in Nairobi. This year, he's going to film the poor areas of the town.

I: Are you going to study at a film school?
PH: No, I'm not. I'm not going to be a film maker. But films can communicate things better than books so I'm going to make films about eccentric New Yorkers and put them online.

Practice

7 Complete the sentences with *be going to.*

1 I want to make a film. I _am going to film_ (film) animals in my city.
2 These films are very personal. _____ (you / put) them on the internet?
3 My parents are going to Mexico. They _____ (make) a documentary about the Aztecs.
4 Paul is busy. He _____ (not watch) the film with us.
5 He uses his camera all the time. He _____ (become) a film director.
6 _____ (you / watch) my film? It's about our town.

➤ LANGUAGE CHOICE 50

8 Match the situations with people's intentions. Use the cues to write sentences.

I'm interested in nature. I'm going to make a film about local birds.

Situations	Intentions
1 I'm interested in nature. *b*	a become a film critic
2 I want to be an actor.	b make a film about local birds
3 I love cinema.	c start acting school next year
4 I'm bored.	d stop watching TV
5 My camera is old.	e watch a thriller
6 I've got no time for my friends.	f buy a new camera

➤ LANGUAGE CHOICE 51

Grammar Alive
Talking about intentions

9 [2.44] Listen to the dialogue. Who is going to do these things, Diane or Pete?

1 make a film *Diane*
2 use a camera
3 lend a camera
4 interview some people

10 Work in pairs. Use the cues to make dialogues.

1 lose all my money yesterday / ask my sister for some

A: *I lost all my money yesterday.*
B: *What are you going to do?*
A: *I'm going to ask my sister for some.*

2 win £100 last week / buy a camera
3 not sleep last night / go to bed early
4 not do the homework last night / tell the teacher
5 break my camera yesterday / take photos with my mobile
6 see my boyfriend/girlfriend with a boy/girl last night / talk to him/her
7 find a bag in the street this morning / give it to the police
8 not remember my mother's birthday / buy her some flowers

11 Write three sentences about your plans for tonight.

I'm going to watch a football game.

12 Work in pairs. Guess your partner's plans for tonight.

A: *Are you going to study?*
B: *No, I'm not.*
A: *Are you going to watch a film?*

Filming unicyclists in New York

65

FILM FANS

Warm Up

1 Work in pairs. Ask and answer the questionnaire on page 118. Is your partner a real film fan?

Listening

2 2.45 2.46 → SKILLS BUILDER 4 Use the strategies in the Skills Builder to listen and match Toby's answers to the questionnaire (a–e) with the topics below (1–6). There is one extra topic.

1 how many films he watches every week
2 the types of films he likes
3 how often he goes to the cinema *a*
4 how many films he's got at home
5 what he does when a film is very slow
6 what he does after a film

3 2.47 2.48 Listen to the complete dialogue. Check your answers to Exercise 2. Is Toby a real film fan? Why/Why not?

4 Look at the Sentence Builder. Which form, *-ing* or infinitive, do we use after *like* and *would like*?

> ### Sentence Builder *like* and *would like*
>
> 1 **Would you like to** do it?
> 2 **I'd like to** go (to the cinema) more often.
> 3 What types of film **do you like** watching?
> 4 **I like** talking about films.

→ LANGUAGE CHOICE 52

5 Use the cues to write questions with *like* or *would like*.

1 like / see / that new French film?

   Would you like to see that new French film?

2 like / watch / foreign films?
3 like / go / to the cinema with me tomorrow?
4 like / talk / about films with your friends?
5 like / eat / popcorn in the cinema?
6 like / watch / a DVD with me?

6 Work in pairs. Ask and answer the questions in Exercise 5.

A: *Do you like watching foreign films?*
B: *No, I don't. I like watching films in my language.*

Reading

7 → SKILLS BUILDER 12 Read the text and use the strategies to choose the best answer to the question.

What is the intention of the writer of the magazine article?

a to give information about the history of the festivals
b to compare two international film festivals
c to give film fans practical information about film festivals
d to review the films at the film festivals

1 Sundance Film Festival 2.49

Where? Park City in the Utah Mountains in January. Film festivals are sometimes tiring but at Sundance you can go skiing between films! The festival started in 1978 with the help of the actor, Robert Redford. Clothes? It's very cold so take warm clothes. It's not very formal in the evenings. Celebrities? A lot of big Hollywood names go to Sundance.
And the films? The best new independent American films – it's easy to get tickets for them.

2 Amazonas Film Festival

Where? Manaus in the Amazon rainforest in Brazil. This festival is in a beautiful, old opera house, the Teatro Amazonas.
Clothes? Informal and relaxed – this is Brazil!
Celebrities? There aren't a lot of big stars but it is a small festival so you can meet stars, like Martin Scorsese, at the hotel swimming pool.
And the films? There are interesting Brazilian, South American and international films. You can watch the films at bus stations in the city and in hospital and prisons. The local people love films and are very friendly so you never get bored at this festival!

3 Cannes Film Festival

Where? The relaxing city of Cannes is in the south of France – it's the oldest and most elegant festival. And you can go to the beach when you are tired!
Clothes? Formal in the evenings – long dresses for women and dinner jackets for men.
Celebrities? Lots! You can see them on the red carpet or in the town's cafés and restaurants. But it's not easy to get an invitation to an exciting celebrity party!
And the films? French, European and international films – but it's difficult to get tickets.

8 Read the article again. Match the people (a–d) with the best festivals for them (1–3). There is one extra person.

a Chris is a real film fan and he loves skiing, too. *1*
b Tom likes horror films and going to capital cities like Paris, London and Berlin.
c Tanya likes films from different countries and is not interested in Hollywood celebrities.
d Karen is more interested in the celebrities than in the films and loves swimming in the sea.

9 Vocabulary Look at the Word Builder and complete it with adjectives in blue from the text. Which type of adjectives (-ed/-ing):

a describes situations or things?
b describes people's feelings?

> **Word Builder** -ed/-ing adjectives
>
> | -ed adjectives | -ing adjectives |
> |---|---|
> | 1 tired | 1 _tiring_ |
> | 2 excited | 2 _____ |
> | 3 _____ | 3 relaxing |
> | 4 interested | 4 _____ |
> | 5 _____ | 5 boring |

LANGUAGE CHOICE 53: VOCABULARY PRACTICE

10 Complete the sentences with the correct form of the words in brackets.

1 I am _interested_ in foreign films. (interest)
2 The film was very _____ . (bore)
3 The action scenes are not very _____ . (excite)
4 I get _____ in films with no action. (bore)
5 I was very _____ after my yoga class. (relax)
6 I was very _____ after my exams. (tire)

11 Film quiz Work in pairs. Student A look at page 117. Student B look at page 119. Choose three questions to ask your partner.

A: *Which city produces the most films?*
B: *Los Angeles.*
A: *No, it's ...*

Your Choice

No Comment

'Why do people need to go out and pay money to see bad films when they can stay at home and see bad television for free?'

Samuel Goldwyn, American film producer

21 GRAMMAR
FILM CREWS

Warm Up

1 Read a conversation with Jake, a camera operator. Tick (✓) the things that he does on the film set.

a use the camera   ☐
b choose the lighting ☐
c move equipment   ☐
d move the camera   ☐

2.50

Q: Jake, you are a camera operator. What exactly do you do?

A: Well, I use the camera and film the scenes. Sometimes I have to decide about the lighting. And of course I have to listen to the director's instructions.

Q: Do you have to move all this equipment?

A: No. The camera operator doesn't have to do a lot of physical work. The crew is usually quite big – some people move the equipment and an assistant has to move the camera.

Q: Do you have to work fast?

A: Yes, we often have to do a lot of things quickly. But I've got a good team and usually we don't have to film one scene many times.

---

have to/not have to

2 Read the sentences (1-5). Match them with the meanings (a-c) below.

1 **Do you have to** work fast? *b*
2 I **have to** decide about the lighting.
3 An assistant **has to** move the camera.
4 We **don't have to** film one scene many times.
5 The camera operator **doesn't have to** do a lot of physical work.

a It's necessary.   b Is it necessary?
c It's not necessary.

3 Use the cues to make sentences about an actor's duties on the film set with (*not*) *have to*.

1 listen to the director

   An actor has to listen to the director.

2 choose his/her clothes
3 learn his/her words
4 move the equipment
5 pay for food and drinks

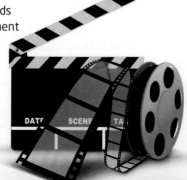

4 Complete the interview with a make-up artist with (*not*) *have to*.

A: What ¹ _do_ you _have to_ do?

B: I ²_____ change the actors' appearance. In horror films and some science fiction films, I ³_____ do a lot of work. In documentaries, I ⁴_____ do a lot - just simple make up.

A: And ⁵_____ you _____ do the actors' hair?

B: No, the hairdresser does it. But she ⁶_____ work with me because the hairstyle and make-up ⁷_____ match.

↪ LANGUAGE CHOICE 54

Grammar Alive
Talking about obligations

5 **2.51** Listen to the dialogue between Tom and his father. Use the cues to talk about Tom's obligations in the school project.

1 find people
   Tom doesn't have to find people.

2 take a camera   4 talk to old people
3 film important places 5 film interviews

6 Work in pairs. Take turns to use the cues to ask and answer questions.

A: *Do you have to make a film?*
B: *I don't have to make a film but I have to take some photos.*

A starts	B answers
1 make a film?	1 take some photos
2 take a camera?	2 make the costumes
3 go to school?	3 work in the library
B starts	**A answers**
4 study a lot?	4 help my sister
5 wear a uniform?	5 wear black trousers
6 do the shopping?	6 clean the bathroom

7 Write four sentences about things you *have to do* and *don't have to do* today.

I have to write an essay. I don't have to go shopping.

Speaking Workshop 7

1 Look at the poster. Choose one of the films to see and give your reasons.

I'd like to see The Social Network *because I use Facebook a lot.*

EXTON FILM CLUB

15 September: *Casablanca* (1942) Director: Michael Curtiz. Starring: Ingrid Bergman and Humphrey Bogart. The most famous romance on film.

29 September: *The Social Network* (2010) Director: David Fincher. Starring: Jesse Eisenberg and Andrew Garfield. About the life of Mark Zuckerburg and how he started Facebook.

12 October: *Pirates of the Caribbean: On Stranger Tides* (2011) Director: Rob Marshall. Starring: Johnny Depp and Penelope Cruz. Captain Sparrow has a new adventure!

2 2.52 DVD 7 **Listen or watch** Look at the photo below. Listen to or watch the dialogue. Match the people: Gary (G), Patsy (P) or both (B) with these opinions.

1 I love old films. *B*
2 My favourite film is *Casablanca*.
3 I like films in 3D.
4 I like films with special effects.
5 I like Johnny Depp.
6 I don't like his new film.

3 Look at the Talk Builder. Which of the replies (a-e) agree or disagree with opinions (1-5)? How do you say the replies in your language?

a: agree

> **Talk Builder** Agreeing and disagreeing
>
> 1 **I love** watching old films.   a **Me too.**
> 2 It's a brilliant film.   b **I don't like it.**
> 3 He's a brilliant actor.   c **That's true**.
> 4 **I don't like** his new film.   d **Me neither.**
> 5 That last film was boring.   e **I don't agree.**
>
> ➡ SKILLS BUILDER 39

4 2.53 **Pronunciation** Listen and repeat the replies. Notice the intonation.

5 Choose the best reply.

1 It's a great film.
  a Me neither.   b Me too.   ⓒ I don't like it.
2 She is a brilliant actress.
  a That's true.   b Me neither.   c Me too.
3 I like romantic films.
  a Me too.   b Me neither.   c Good idea.
4 I don't like old films.
  a Me too.   b Me neither.   c Okay.

6 Speaking Work in pairs. Give your opinions about recent films. Agree and disagree.

A: Prometheus *is a great film.*
B: *That's true.*

7 Work in pairs. Discuss films and make a list of your top five films.

➡ SKILLS BUILDER 39

1 Choose five of your favourite films. Write notes about them.

  • name of film   • type of film
  • director   • starring
  • actors   • about

2 Tell your partner about your films. Agree and disagree with his/her opinions.

3 Agree on a list of your top five films.

Writing Workshop 4

DARTFORD SHORT FILM FESTIVAL

We are organising a competition next year on 20–22 May for local amateur film makers. There are some great prizes for the winners!

Our website is opening on 10 March and you can upload your videos at www.dartfordfilmclub.com or send your DVD to 3, Drayton Place, Dartford.
For more information contact dartfordfilm@zmail.com.
(before 10 March)

1 Look at the poster. Which of this information does it give?

a the dates of the competition
b the types of films in the competition
c how much it costs to enter the competition
d where you can send your films
e the prizes for the winners
f where you can get more information
g what clothes to wear at the festival

2 Read the email. Which of the information in Exercise 1 does Freya ask about?

1 Dear Sir/Madam,
2 I am writing to ask for information about your film competition. I am seventeen and I make skateboarding videos. I also film basketball matches. I would like to make music videos, too.
3 I would like to ask about the films. What types of films do you accept? Do you accept music and sports videos? How long does my film have to be?
4 I would also like more information about the competition. How much does it cost to enter and what is the closing date to send in films? I would like to ask about the prizes, too. Are there prizes for different age groups and for different types of films?

I look forward to hearing from you.
5 Yours faithfully,
Freya Williams

Text Builder

3 Match the parts of the email (1-5) in Exercise 2 with the headings (a-e).

a the reason for writing and personal information
b more questions   c begin a letter formally
d questions about films   e end a letter formally

4 Look at the sentences from the email. How do you say the linkers, in blue, in your language? Find more examples in the email.

I make skateboarding videos.
I *also* film basketball matches.
I would like to make music videos, *too*.

5 Use the words in brackets to rewrite the second sentences.

1 I make documentaries. I film animals. (also)
I also film animals.
2 I would like information about prices. I have got some questions about dates. (too)
3 I play football. I like swimming and running. (also)
4 My sister watches a lot of films at home. She goes to the cinema a lot. (too)

6 Write an email to ask for information.

→ SKILLS BUILDER 24

1 **Choose one of the advertisements (a-c).**

a **New school film club starting next week! Some great films!**

b Cheap Zumba classes! Great teacher and small groups!

c **School music competition on 15 June. Some great prizes!**

2 **Write four or five questions to ask about the advertisement.**

• when?   • where?   • how much?
• who?   • what (prizes/films)?

3 **Use your questions to write a formal email asking for information. Include some personal information.**

7 Work in pairs. Read your partner's email. Check it for spelling, punctuation and grammar/vocabulary mistakes.

8 FOOD AND DRINK

Objectives: Listen, read and **talk about** food; **order** food and drink in a café; **learn more about** the future tense and zero conditionals.

TOPIC TALK

1 Look at the photos (a-l) and the network. What food can you see in the photos?

2 3.1 3.2 Listen to Toby (1) and Chris (2) talking about food. Which of them eats the healthiest food? Give examples.

3 3.3 3.4 Listen again to the first person. Complete the information in the network.

My food

I usually eat a lot of [1] _meat_ and [2] _____ .
I don't eat a lot of [3] _____ .
I drink a lot of [4] _____ .
My favourite meal is [5] breakfast/lunch/dinner.
I often eat snacks, like [6] _____ .

Fruit: apple, banana, cherry, kiwi, lemon, melon, orange, pear, strawberry, tomato
Vegetables: beans, broccoli, cabbage, carrot, cucumber, lettuce, mushroom, onion, potato
Cereals: bread, (breakfast) cereal, rice, pasta
Meat: beef, chicken, lamb, pork sausages
Fish: salmon, sardines, tuna
Dairy: cheese, yoghurt

Drinks: coffee, cola, fruit juice (orange/lemon), milk, tea, water

Snacks: biscuits, cakes, chocolate, crisps, fruit, ice cream, nuts, popcorn, sweets

4 3.5 Pronunciation Listen and <u>underline</u> the words in the network. Listen again and repeat them.

vegetables

LANGUAGE CHOICE 55: VOCABULARY PRACTICE

5 Work in pairs. Use the network to tell your partner about the food you eat. How healthy is your partner's diet?

a

Warm Up

1 **Your Culture** Look at the photos (a-c). Which dishes are popular in your country? What traditional dishes do people eat?

2 Read the interview. Which opinions do you agree with?

Predictions *will/won't*

3 Read the sentences from the text and complete the rule.

Affirmative	
Meat **will be** more expensive.	
Negative	
Fast food **won't** disappear.	
Italians **won't** stop eating pasta.	

Questions	Short answers
Will we all **eat** the same dishes?	Yes, they **will**. / No, they **won't**.
Will we **go** to restaurants?	Yes, we **will**. / No, we **won't**.
What **will** they **cook**?	

- We use *will* and *won't* to talk about the *present/future*.

4 Add two future time expressions from the text to the list.

- tomorrow
- in two weeks' time, in six months' time, _____
- next week, next month, _____

Food and Drink

EATING IN THE FUTURE

Interviewer: Our eating habits change all th[e] time. What will people eat in ten years' time[?]

Expert: There will be less food around and some peop[le] will eat very little. Meat and fish will be more expensive s[o] there will be more vegetarians.

I: Will we buy more vitamins?

E: Yes, we will. We will probably take more vitamins and minerals because there won't be a lot of them in our food.

I: What will happen to fast food?

E: Oh, fast food won't disappear because our lifestyle w[ill] be very fast. But it will change – we'll buy salads and fresh sandwiches, not chips and burgers.

I: Will we go to restaurants?

E: Yes, we will but home-cooking will be more popular because it's cheaper.

I: What will people cook?

E: It's difficult to say. This year, Japanese food is the mos[t] popular because it's quick and healthy but this fashio[n] will probably change. Maybe next year we'll eat South[...] American food.

I: Will we all eat the same dishes?

E: No, we won't. Food is an important part of our culture and people will always eat their traditional local dishes[.] Italians will always eat pasta and the Japanese will always eat sushi. Some things won't change.

Practice

5 Complete the predictions for 2020 with *will* or *won't*. Use the interview to help you.

1 People _*will*_ eat fast food.
2 Cafés _____ sell unhealthy food.
3 Salads _____ become more popular.
4 Italians _____ forget pizza.
5 Vitamins _____ be less popular.
6 People _____ invite friends to their home.
7 Our lifestyle _____ become slower.

 LANGUAGE CHOICE 56

6 Use the cues to make questions about the future of food.

1 food / be more expensive?

   Will food be more expensive?

2 Italian food / still be popular?
3 fast food restaurants / disappear?
4 people / eat a lot of sweets?
5 our national food / become popular in the world?
6 people / stop eating meat?
7 traditional dishes / change?
8 young people / cook at home?

7 Work in pairs. Ask and answer the questions from Exercise 6.

A: *Will food be more expensive?*
B: *Yes, it will.*

8 Read the situations. Use the cues to write predictions about the future.

1 People are interested in foreign food. (learn to cook foreign dishes, ethnic restaurants not disappear)

   We will learn to cook foreign dishes. Ethnic restaurants won't disappear.

2 Restaurants are expensive. (not go out very often, learn to cook at home)
3 A lot of people are overweight. (schools not sell sweets, children drink more water)
4 People want to live longer. (eat more fruit and vegetables, hamburgers not be popular)

LANGUAGE CHOICE 57

Grammar Alive
Predicting the future

9 3.7 Listen to a conversation at a fortune-teller's. List five predictions about Janet's future. Which ones would you like to be true for you?

   1 *She will become a chef.*

10 Work in pairs. Use the cues to ask and answer about your future.

A: *Will I have a lot of money?*
B: *No, you won't but you'll be happy.*

A starts	B answers
1 have a lot of money?	1 be happy
2 get married?	2 fall in love many times
3 travel a lot?	3 have a beautiful home
4 have an interesting job?	4 do an important job
5 be famous?	5 be popular

B starts	A answers
6 be a scientist?	6 be a science teacher
7 live in a different country?	7 travel a lot
8 have a family?	8 have a lot of friends
9 have a lot of adventures?	9 live long
10 fall in love?	10 meet a lot of interesting people

11 Now make three predictions about your partner's future. Discuss them in pairs.

A: *You'll study in the USA.*
B: *No, I won't. / That's great.*

23 SKILLS
GOOD FOOD

Warm Up

1 **Where are your fruit and vegetables from? Use the list below.**

We eat oranges from Spain. Our apples come from our garden!

- my garden
- my country
- a different continent
- my local area
- a foreign country

Reading

2 **Read the article. Match the topics (a–d) with the paragraphs (1–3). There is one extra topic.**

a animals on roofs   c a roof garden
b healthy food   d a good idea

3 → SKILLS BUILDER 13 **Use the strategies to match words in blue in the text with these meanings:**

1 the top part of a building *roof*
2 with no synthetic chemicals etc.
3 female birds that produce eggs to eat
4 it is sweet and bees make it
5 to produce food from plants
6 this gas changes our climate
7 insects that make honey
8 a person who buys a house or shop

4 **Read the article again. Choose the best answer (a–d) to these questions.**

1 Where did Azul-Valerie want to grow food?
  a in London parks   c in roof gardens
  b in people's gardens   d in a supermarket

2 What kind of food is her project producing?
  a eggs and honey   c fresh, organic food
  b cheap fruit and vegetables   d unhealthy food

3 Why is the food good for the planet?
  a it is local and organic   c it is not expensive
  b it is fresh   d it creates CO_2

4 What do they do with the eggs from the hens in East London?
  a sell them in supermarkets   c eat them at home
  b give them to people   d make omelettes with them

5 What kind of shop is Fortnum & Mason?
  a an organic supermarket   c a famous food shop
  b a cheap food shop   d a small food shop

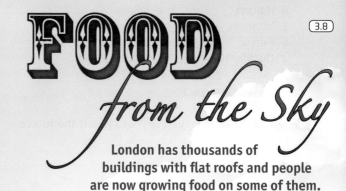

FOOD
from the Sky

(3.8)

London has thousands of buildings with flat roofs and people are now growing food on some of them. Anita Morgan reports.

1 Azul-Valerie Thorne lived in a small village. When she moved to London, she had a good idea – to grow fruit and vegetables on the roofs of buildings. Azul-Valerie met the owner of a North London supermarket and they started a project called *Food from the Sky*.

2 Now, local people help in the roof garden and grow organic fruit and vegetables. For example, a group of students from a local school are growing mushrooms. People also go there to learn about urban gardening and there are a lot of interesting birds and insects on the roof. The project sells the fresh food in the supermarket; it is not cheap but it is very popular. The food is healthy and good for the planet because it is organic and does not have to travel. A lot of fresh fruit and vegetables in British supermarkets come from Africa or South America and this makes a lot of CO_2.

5 Vocabulary Look at the sentences in the Word Builder. Match the words (1–4) in **bold** with the words below (a–j). Use the network in the Topic Talk on page 71 to help you.

a cheese omelette   **b** ~~biscuits~~   **c** dinner   **d** sushi   **e** meat
f pizza   **g** lunch   **h** vegetables   **i** fish   **j** breakfast

> **Word Builder** Confusing words
>
> 1 I often eat **snacks** like crisps and biscuits. *b*
> 2 My favourite **meal** is Sunday lunch.
> 3 Lasagne is a typical Italian **dish**.
> 4 They started a project called **Food** from the Sky.

 LANGUAGE CHOICE 58: VOCABULARY PRACTICE

3 There are similar projects to produce organic food with hens and bees. The roof of an old factory in East London has hens and downstairs there is a café with fantastic omelettes because of the fresh eggs from the roof. Fortnum & Mason, the most famous and expensive food shop in London, has bees on its roof in Piccadilly. It sells the honey in the shop; it is expensive but very good. You can visit the bees or watch them on a special webcam.

Writing

6 Look at the Sentence Builder. How do you say the words in **bold** in your language?

> **Sentence Builder** *because/because of*
>
> 1 The food is good for the planet **because** it is organic. (*because* + sentence)
>
> 2 There is a café with fantastic omelettes **because of** the fresh eggs. (*because of* + noun)
>
> ➔ SKILLS BUILDER 25

7 Use the cues to write sentences.

1 supermarkets / good for / roof gardens / their flat roofs
   Supermarkets are good for roof gardens because of their flat roofs.

2 those vegetables / fresh / they come from / our garden
3 omelettes in that café / good / the fresh eggs
4 that honey / expensive / it comes from Fortnum & Mason
5 we / not go / to that restaurant / the prices
6 that market / good / the vegetables are cheap

 LANGUAGE CHOICE 59

8 Work in pairs. Choose six questions to ask your partner.

1 How much fresh food do you eat?
2 Do you ever eat organic food? Why/ Why not?
3 How often do you eat fast food?
4 How often do you eat snacks?
5 What is your biggest meal of the day?
6 What time do you have dinner?
7 What is your favourite dish from your country?
8 What is your favourite international dish?
9 Where does your family buy food?
10 How often do you help with the food shopping?

9 Tell the class some of your answers.

Monica eats fast food once a week. Her family buys food at the local market.

Your Choice

> **No Comment**
>
> 'I don't eat snails. I prefer fast food.'
>
> *Roger Von Oech,* American inventor

Warm Up

1 Look at the photo and name the foods (a-e). Which ones do you like?

c: garlic

2 Read the text. Which of the things below are good (+) and which are bad (-) for us? Can you add more foods?

• biscuits • fish • tomatoes • fruit

(3.9)

This week's nutrition tips.

1 Eat five or six times a day. If you are hungry, you feel moody and you can't concentrate.

2 Popular snacks, like crisps or biscuits, aren't healthy. If we eat a lot of these foods, we have problems with our weight. Choose healthy snacks, like fruit.

3 Cook your meals at home from fresh products. If you use fresh products, your meals don't have a lot of bad chemicals and are healthier.

4 Fish is good for the brain. When you don't eat fish, your memory gets worse.

5 Broccoli and tomatoes have a lot of vitamins and minerals. They help us to stay healthy if we eat them regularly.

---

3 Which of the things from the text do you do?

Present Conditional

4 Read the sentences (1-2) from the text. What do they do (a or b)?

1 *If you **are** hungry, you **feel** moody.*
2 *Tomatoes **help** us to stay healthy **if** we **eat** them regularly.*

a describe a rule
b predict the future

---

5 Read the sentence from the text and complete the pattern.

*If/When you **don't eat** fish, your memory **gets** worse.*

• *if/when* + Present Simple tense, _____ tense.

6 Use the cues to make conditional sentences.

1 you not drink enough water → feel tired
   If you don't drink enough water, you feel tired.
2 children eat a lot of sweets → have problems with weight
3 you not sleep eight hours every night → feel moody
4 eat chocolate → feel happy
5 not eat fruit and vegetables → have health problems

➡ LANGUAGE CHOICE 60

Grammar Alive Talking about habits

7 (3.10) Listen to the interview with a teenager. What does he eat when:

1 he leaves school?
2 he goes out?
3 his mother cooks?
4 he is at home alone?

8 Work in pairs. Use the cues to make dialogues.

A: *What do you do if there is no food at home?*
B: *If there is no food at home, I go shopping.*

A starts	B answers
1 there is no food at home?	1 go shopping
2 your guests be vegetarian?	2 make a salad
3 want to lose weight?	3 eat more vegetables

B starts	A answers
4 want to cook dinner?	4 look in a cook book
5 your friends be hungry?	5 cook for them
6 not like the food in a restaurant?	6 not eat it

9 Finish the sentences to say something true about you.

1 If I am tired, _____ .
2 If I feel hungry, _____ .
3 If I feel happy, _____ .

Speaking Workshop 8

1 Look at the menu. What would you like for lunch or dinner today? Tell the class.

I'd like fish and chips and an orange juice.

Main dishes
Fish and chips £4.50
Egg, sausage and chips £4.00
Cheeseburger (small/big)
£3.00/£5.00
Small/large/giant pizza
£3.00/£5.00/£6.00

Today's specials
Lamb curry £5.50
Vegetable lasagne £4.00
Tuna salad (small/big)
£4.50/£5.00
Chicken salad (small/big)
£3.50/£4.50

Sandwiches
Cheese and tomato £2.25
Chicken £2.50
Tuna £2.50

Drinks
Cola (small/big) £1.20/£2.50
Orange juice £2.50
Milk £2.50
Bottle of water £1.50
Small/regular/big coffee
(white/black/cappuccino/latte)
£2.50/£3.00/£3.50
Tea £2.00

2 **3.11** **DVD 8** Listen or watch Listen to or watch the dialogue. Which of the things from the menu above do Zac and Michelle order?

3 **3.11** **DVD 8** Listen or watch Listen to or watch the dialogue again. Are the sentences true (T) or false (F)?

1 There is no vegetable lasagne. *F*
2 Zac is hungry because they danced a lot last night.
3 Michelle wants to eat healthy food.
4 Michelle is interested in football.
5 Michelle is really very hungry.
6 Zac is very angry with Michelle.

4 Look at the Talk Builder. Who says the sentences A, B and C, the customers or the waiter?

Talk Builder At a café

A: Hello, **can I help you**? *waiter*
B: **What have you got** for lunch?
A: **Here's the menu. I'm sorry there's no** lamb curry.
C: **I'd like** a large pizza, please.
A: **What would you like**?
B: For me, a small tuna salad, **please**.
A: **What would you like to drink**?
B: A small bottle of water **for me, please**.
C: A large cola **for me, please**.
B: **How much is that**?
A: **That's** thirteen pounds fifty, please.
B: **Here you are**.
A: **Thanks**.

→ SKILLS BUILDER 40

5 **3.12** Pronunciation Listen and repeat the questions. Notice the polite intonation.

6 Speaking Work in pairs. Complete the dialogue. Then act it out and change the words in italics.

A: Can I ¹ _help_ you?
B: Yes, what have you got for *lunch*?
A: Here's the ² _____ . I'm sorry, there's no *pizza*. What would you ³ _____ ?
B: I'd like *a big cheeseburger*, ⁴ _____ .
A: What would you like to ⁵ _____ ?
B: An *orange juice* for ⁶ _____ , please.

7 Work in groups. Act out a situation at a café.

→ SKILLS BUILDER 40

1 Look at the menu in Exercise 1. Add three more of your favourite dishes to it.
   spaghetti / chicken kebab / paella

2 Choose three things from the menu: a drink, and something to eat. Practise asking for them.

3 Work in groups of three. Choose one person to be the waiter/waitress. Use the Talk Builder to act out the situation.

8 What did you choose to eat and drink? Tell the class.

I chose a giant pizza and an orange juice.

Language Review Modules 7 and 8

1 Films/Food **Choose the correct words to complete the texts.**

My ¹*favourite/brilliant* film is *Troy*. The ²*special/action* effects are fantastic. I also like ³*animations/thrillers,* like *Shrek* because they've got funny ⁴*dramas/ dialogues.*
I want to be healthy so I don't eat a lot of ⁵*meat/fruit.* I eat ⁶*cereals/vegetables,* like broccoli and carrots. I don't eat unhealthy ⁷*meals/snacks,* like crisps. My favourite ⁸*dish/food* is lasagne. I often eat dairy products, like ⁹*cheese/bread* and I drink a lot of fresh ¹⁰*cola/juice.*   /10

2 *-ed/-ing* adjectives **Complete the text with the correct forms of the words in brackets.**

The last Tarantino film was not very ¹¹_____ (interest). I got really ¹²_____ (tire) because the dialogue was ¹³_____ (bore) and the action was not ¹⁴_____ (excite). I was more ¹⁵_____ (interest) in the music.   /5

3 *like* and *would like* **Complete the sentences with *like* or *would like.***

16 I _____ to visit India next year.
17 _____ you _____ eating in restaurants?
18 _____ you _____ to see my photos?
19 I _____ watching films in the cinema.   /4

4 *also, too/because, because of* **Use the words in brackets to rewrite the sentences.**

20 I like Italian restaurants. I cook Italian food. (also)
21 I often go to the cinema. I watch DVDs. (too)
22 Everyone loves this café. They've got fantastic cakes. (because of)
23 He made his last film in New Zealand. There are beautiful mountains there. (because)   /4

5 *be going to* **Use the cues to write sentences about people's intentions.**

24 My parents / buy a new car
25 Jane / make a film about Venice?
26 I / not spend the summer in the city
27 Mike / cook lunch at home
28 you / watch this film?   /5

6 *will/won't* **Use the cues to write predictions.**

29 Cinema tickets / be very expensive
30 People / not go to the cinema
31 DVDs / disappear
32 people / watch all films online?
33 cinemas / exist?   /5

7 *have to/not have to* **Complete the text with *have to* or *not have to.***

Restaurant chefs have an interesting job. They ³⁴_____ know a lot of different dishes. They ³⁵_____ create the restaurant's menu. They can sleep in the morning because they ³⁶_____ come to the restaurant before twelve o'clock. In the kitchen they ³⁷_____ wear a uniform but they ³⁸_____ do boring jobs, like cleaning.   /5

8 Present Conditional **Complete the Present Conditional sentences with the correct forms of the verbs in brackets.**

39 If people _____ (work) too much, they _____ (feel) depressed.
40 If parents _____ (not cook) at home, their children _____ (eat) more fast food.
41 If children _____ (not do) sport, they _____ (feel) sleepy and tired.   /5

9 Agreeing and disagreeing/At a café **Choose the correct words to complete the dialogue.**

A: Let's look at the ⁴²*meal/menu.* There are a lot of different sandwiches.
B: I don't like sandwiches.
A: ⁴³*Me neither./I don't agree.* Salads are healthier.
B: ⁴⁴*I agree./Me too.*
Waiter: Hello. What would you like?
B: A tuna salad, please.
A: And ⁴⁵*please/for me* a chicken salad.
Waiter: What would you like ⁴⁶*to drink/for lunch*?
A: Water for me, please. ⁴⁷*How much is that?/Can I help you?*
Waiter: That's sixteen pounds fifty.
B: ⁴⁸*Here you are./Please.*   /7

Self Assessment

3.13 Listen and check your answers. Write down your scores. Use the table to find practice exercises.

Exercise	If you need practice, go to
1	Language Choice 49, 55
2	Language Choice 53
3	Language Choice 52
4	Language Choice 59; SB p.70 ex.4, 5
5	Language Choice 50, 51
6	Language Choice 56, 57
7	Language Choice 54
8	Language Choice 60
9	SB p.69 ex.3; SB p.77 ex.4

LEARNING LINKS: 1 Read and listen to the film review in **Culture Choice 4** on page 103. Then do a project about a film from your country.
2 Exam Choice 4 → My Lab / Workbook pages 88-89.
3 Check Your Progress 8 → MyLab / Workbook page 90. Complete the Module Diary.

9 COUNTRIES

AIR MAIL

Objectives: Listen, read, write and **talk about** countries; **ask for** and **give** directions; **make suggestions**; **write** a postcard; **learn more** about articles and pronouns.

a China

b Brazil

TOPIC TALK

① Look at the network and the photos (a–c). Guess answers to these questions about the countries in the photos.

1 Which country is the largest?
2 Which country has the biggest population?
3 Which country has a capital city called Pretoria?
4 In which country is it usually hot and dry?
5 Which country has got thousands of great beaches?

② `3.14` `3.15` Listen to three descriptions. Check your guesses from Exercise 1.

③ `3.16` `3.17` Listen again to the first description. Complete the information in the network.

④ `3.18` Pronunciation Listen to words from the network and <u>underline</u> the stress.

population

➤ **LANGUAGE CHOICE 61: VOCABULARY PRACTICE**

⑤ Work in pairs. Use the network to talk about *your* country. Do you agree about the facts?

c South Africa

My country

My country is ¹(*very*)/*quite* big.
The population is ²_____ million.
Our capital city is ³_____ .
In the ⁴_____ , it is often quite
⁵_____ and ⁶_____ .
In the ⁷_____ , there are some lovely
⁸_____ .

Seasons
spring, summer, autumn, winter
Weather
cloudy, cold, dry, foggy, hot, icy, rainy, snowy, sunny, windy

east/west, north/south, centre
- - - - - - - - - - - - - - - - -
beaches, forests, lakes, mountains, national parks

79

25 GRAMMAR
ABROAD

Warm Up

1 Look at the photo. Would you like to study abroad? Where would you like to go? Why?

2 Read what Chinese students say about their student life in the USA. Which things are difficult for them? Why?

- finding friends
- parties
- learning maths
- food

a/an/the

3 Look at the words in blue in the text and complete the rules.

- We use *a/an* in front of a vowel (*apple*). We use *a/an* in front of a consonant (*hamburger*).
- We *use/don't use a* or *an* in front of singular countable nouns (*friend, essay*).
- We *use/don't use a* or *an* in front of uncountable and plural nouns (*politics, conversations*).

4 Read the sentences (1-4) from the text and the meanings (a-b) below. Circle the correct word, *a* or *the*.

1 *There are thousands of students from around **the world**.*
2 *I'd like to have **a friend**.*
3 *I have dinner in **a local Chinese restaurant**.*
4 ***The teacher** says I am his best student.*

a one of many people/things: *a/the*
b a unique or specific person/thing: *a/the*

5 The expressions below don't have *a* or *the*. Complete the list with expressions in red in the text.

1 at school, at college, *at university* , at _____
2 have breakfast, have lunch, have _____
3 go to school, go to work, go _____
4 for _____ , for lunch, for dinner

(3.19)

There are thousands of students from around the world at American universities. Read some Chinese students' opinions about their life in the USA.

'It is difficult to make friends here. I'd like to have an American friend but they only talk about boring things, like eating or sleeping and tell jokes. Serious topics, like philosophy or politics are not 'cool'. I know a lot of people at university but I haven't got American friends. Actually, a lot of Chinese students go home after classes and go out with their Chinese friends.' **Li**

'I like the parties here and I think American students are friendly but ... I don't like American food. At the beginning, I had cornflakes for breakfast and a hamburger for lunch and dinner. I felt horrible. Now I cook at home or have dinner in a local Chinese restaurant.' **Mei**

'I am really good at maths and ICT and the teachers here are great. The teacher says I am his best student and I'm learning a lot. But some subjects are very difficult because I have to read and write in English. Now I have to write an essay for my philosophy class so I am studying a lot.' **Kang**

Practice

6 Complete the text with *a/an* or -.

I come from Poland but now I am ¹ _a_ student in Ireland. I study ² _____ Irish history and ³ _____ culture. I joined ⁴ _____ drama club and I'm learning to be ⁵ _____ actor. I am living with ⁶ _____ friend in ⁷ _____ small flat but we want to move to ⁸ _____ bigger house with some Irish friends. We don't spend a lot of money: we walk to ⁹ _____ college and we cook our meals at ¹⁰ _____ home.

➤ LANGUAGE CHOICE 62

7 Complete the sentences with *a/an* or *the*.

1 Is there _a_ cathedral in London?
2 Moscow is _____ capital of Russia.
3 Luxembourg is _____ very small country but it's got _____ airport.
4 I love Brazil. _____ people are very friendly.
5 _____ climate in Scandinavia is very cold: in winter _____ temperature is -40°C.

8 Complete the dialogue with *a/an* or *the*.

A: Jim, where is ¹ _the_ Spanish dictionary? I'm writing ² _____ essay in Spanish and I need it.
B: It's in ³ _____ living room. I watched ⁴ _____ film in Spanish and I wanted to look up some words.
A: What did you watch?
B: Oh, it was ⁵ _____ old film by Buñuel. Our teacher shows us a lot of Spanish films.
A: That's nice, you've got ⁶ _____ good teacher. Did you understand ⁷ _____ dialogue?
B: I understood ⁸ _____ story but ⁹ _____ actors spoke very fast so it was hard to understand.

➤ LANGUAGE CHOICE 63

Grammar Alive Asking about places

9 🔊 3.20 Listen to the conversation between two students and complete the sentences with the places. Use correct articles.

1 Chen is looking for _the office_ .
2 Jason shows her _____ and _____ .
3 Jason invites Chen to _____ .
4 Chen wants to go to _____ and the _____ first.

10 Work in pairs. It is your first day at a university. Use the cues to ask and answer questions about the campus.

A: *Is there a swimming pool?*
B: *No, there isn't but the swimming pool in town is not far from here.*

A starts	B answers
1 swimming pool?	1 swimming pool in town – not far from here
2 shopping centre?	2 supermarket – open 24 hours
3 student club?	3 disco – open every night
4 restaurant?	4 café – has got very good food

B starts	A answers
5 bookshop?	5 library – very good
6 cinema?	6 film club – meets every Friday
7 sports centre?	7 gym – open from 6 a.m. to 10 p.m.
8 clothes shop?	8 town – has got lots of good shops

11 Take turns to make sentences about these things in your school.

The students are very nice. The equipment is new and very modern. The food in the canteen is quite good.

classrooms   equipment   library   sports centre
café   computer lab   students   teachers

COSTA RICA

Home   Favourites   Features   Travel   Hotels

MONTEVERDE
NATURE RESERVE
SAN JOSÉ
Irazu
TORTUGUERO
NATIONAL PARK
CARIBBEAN SEA
CARTAGO
CAHUITA
NATIONAL PARK
PUERTO VIEJO
PACIFIC OCEAN
OO 25 50 75 100
kms
CORCOVADO
NATIONAL PARK

3.21

Introducing Costa Rica

Costa Rica has beautiful beaches, amazing animals and friendly people. You can walk in a rainforest, go hiking up an active volcano, go white-water rafting on a mountain river and swim or surf in the Pacific and Caribbean. Two million tourists visit this small Central American country every year and Costa Rica is the world's best place for eco-tourism with thirty-two national parks.

Warm Up

1 Vocabulary **Look at the map of Costa Rica and the vocabulary box below. Guess which sentences are true.**

1 Costa Rica is in Central America. *T*
2 The capital is Puerto Viejo.
3 Costa Rica is a big country.
4 It is a good place for a holiday.
5 It has got interesting animals and birds.
6 It has got a lot of national parks.

Fast Facts

Population: 4 million
Area: 51,000 sq km (30% is protected)
Animals: monkeys, sloths, sea turtles and lots of birds
Happy and green: Costa Rica is first in the Happy Planet Index. It has the happiest people and is one of the 'greenest' countries in the world.
Climate: The winter season is from May to October. It rains a lot and is very hot. The summer is from November to April and it is sunny and dry.
Coffee: This is the national drink and is the best coffee in the world.

Travel

Animals
see crocodiles, elephants, giraffes, lions, monkeys, sloths, turtles

Transport
go by bike, bus, car, plane

Activities
go hiking, sightseeing, surfing, swimming, white-water rafting

➡ LANGUAGE CHOICE 64:
VOCABULARY PRACTICE

Travellers' Blogs

Puerto Viejo

We are relaxing here on the Caribbean. Puerto Viejo is a party and surf town so we love it! We go to the beach every morning by bike (they are cheap to rent). Yesterday, we went to the Cahuita National Park – the monkeys are amazing and I took some great photos!
fionaGH read more

Leaving Costa Rica

I am in San José, the capital, and I am leaving tomorrow. The best things in my three weeks here? White-water rafting on the Pacuare River and visiting Tortuguero National Park by boat – I saw the sea turtles. They're really cool.
eriktheblue read more

Reading

2 Read the travel website and check your guesses from Exercise 1.

3 Work in pairs. Read the article and complete the notes.

A:
Where? [1] *Central America*
National drink: [2] _____
Things you can do: [3] _____
Animals you can see: [4] _____

B:
Population: [1] *4 million*
Type of tourism: [2] _____
Places you can visit: [3] _____
Best time to go: [4] _____

4 Work in pairs. Use the headings in Exercise 3 to ask and answer questions about Costa Rica.

B: *Where is Costa Rica?*
A: *It's in Central America.*

5 What would you like to do in Costa Rica? Tell the class.

I'd like to go white-water rafting on the Pacuare River and ...

6 3.22 Vocabulary Complete the Word Builder with adjectives. Then listen and check your answers. Add more nationalities to the groups.

Italian, Argentinian, Russian, Serbian, Colombian

Word Builder Nationality adjectives

Country/Continent	Adjective
Costa Rica	1 *Costa Rican*
America	2 _____
Canada	3 _____
Britain	British
Spain	4 _____
Turkey	5 _____
Poland	6 _____
Japan	7 _____
China	8 _____
Greece	9 _____
France	10 _____

→ LANGUAGE CHOICE 65: VOCABULARY PRACTICE

7 Work in pairs. Ask and answer questions about the people below. Ask more questions about famous people you like. Check your answers on p.117.

A: *What nationality is Lionel Messi?*
B: *Is he Italian?*
A: *No, he's Argentinian but he lives in Barcelona.*

- Lionel Messi (footballer) • Maria Sharapova (tennis player)
- Kobe Bryant (basketball player) • Jesse Eisenberg (actor)
- Sebastian Vettel (racing driver) • Penelope Cruz (actress)
- Shakira (singer) • JK Rowling (writer)

Listening

8 3.23 3.24 Listen to a dialogue about Costa Rica. Answer the questions.

1 When did Lucy go to Costa Rica?
   She went to Costa Rica last January.
2 How long did she go for?
3 How did she travel around Costa Rica?
4 What were her favourite animals?
5 What weather did she have on holiday?
6 What adventure activities and sports did she do?

9 3.23 3.24 → SKILLS BUILDER 5 Use the strategies to listen to the dialogue. Match the people, Adam and Lucy, with their intentions (1-4).

1 wants information about a place *Adam*
2 wants to help the other person
3 wants to read the other person's book
4 wants to talk about a holiday in the past

10 Your Culture Work in pairs. Choose three things about your country and write notes about them.

a things to do
   things to do - go sightseeing in London, go hiking in Scotland
b things to see
c animals to see
d places to visit
e best time to go

11 Work in pairs. Ask and answer questions about your country.

A: *When is the best time to visit?*
B: *In the summer. That's from June to September. It's hot and sunny.*

Your Choice

No Comment

'Before you travel, organise your clothes and money. Take half your clothes and twice the money.'

Susan Heller

EUROPEAN TOUR

Europe in fifteen days

✓ Explore Europe!
✓ Visit ten countries in two weeks!
✓ See the most beautiful cities of the Old Continent: London, Amsterdam, Vienna, Rome, Paris, Barcelona and more.

Warm Up

1 Read the advertisement. Would you like to go on the tour? Why/Why not?

2 Read the dialogue between two tourists on a tour of Europe. Where are they? Why do they think they are in Germany?

(3.25)

Bill: Mike, can you see our guide anywhere?
Mike: No, I can't see anyone from our group. I think we are lost.
Bill: Where are we?
Mike: Somewhere in Germany, I think. Everyone is speaking German and there are German cars everywhere - Volkswagens, Mercedes.
Bill: Let's ask someone. Can you say anything in German?
Mike: Well, 'danke' ... it means 'thanks' I think. But it's not very useful now.
Bill: Well, we've got nothing to do so let's go to this café and eat something. Let's look at the menu. Oh, no, everything is in German.
Mike: Look at that sign! Vienna 50 km! We're in Austria!
Bill: That's strange! No one mentioned Austria.

someone, anyone, everyone, no one

3 Complete the table with the words in blue from the text.

words with negative meaning	nowhere, _nothing_ , 1_____
words used in questions and negative sentences	anywhere, 2_____ , 3_____
words referring to **all** things/people/places	everywhere, 4_____ , 5_____
words referring to **some** things/people/places	somewhere, 6_____ , 7_____

4 Complete the sentences with the words from Exercise 3.

1 Italy is great – _everyone_ is very friendly.
2 Speak Spanish! _____ speaks French here.
3 Where is my passport? I can't find it _____ .
4 In Paris there are tourists _____!
5 Spain is beautiful. I loved _____ there.
6 When I first went to India, I didn't know _____ about Indian culture.

↘ LANGUAGE CHOICE 66

5 Complete the text with the words from Exercise 3.

Some years ago, I went to Rome. I stayed in a hotel ¹ _somewhere_ near the Coliseum. I didn't know ² _____ in Rome so I went ³ _____ alone. I didn't have ⁴ _____ to do in the evenings so I went for long walks.
One day, I saw a girl. She was very pretty and ⁵ _____ in the street looked at her. She saw me – she smiled and said ⁶ _____ in Italian. I didn't understand her but ⁷ _____ said to me: 'You're lucky! She wants to meet you here tomorrow.'
It was a long time ago but I remember ⁸ _____ – her green eyes, her dark hair and her smile. We got married and today is our anniversary!

Grammar Alive Suggestions

6 (3.26) Listen to the dialogue. Make a list of Steve's suggestions. Which suggestion does Jim like?

7 Work in pairs. Use the cues to make dialogues. Give negative answers.

A: *Let's watch something interesting.*
B: *There's nothing interesting on TV.*

A starts	B answers
1 watch – interesting	1 on TV
2 drink – hot	2 in the bar
3 eat – vegetarian	3 on the menu
4 see – famous	4 in this hotel

B starts	A answers
5 go out with – attractive	5 in our school
6 read – exciting	6 in the library
7 talk to – intelligent	7 at this party
8 listen – good	8 on the radio

SKILLS
Speaking Workshop 9

1 Look at the map on page 119. Work in pairs. Ask and answer these questions.

1 Which café is next to the station?

The Green Parrot Café.

2 Which cafés are near to the swimming pool?
3 Which café is next to the sports centre?
4 Which café is near to the cinema?

2 **3.27** **DVD 9** Listen or watch Listen to or watch the dialogue. Follow Sean's route on the map on page 119 from A to the café.

3 **3.27** **DVD 9** Listen or watch Listen to or watch the dialogue again. Match the people (1–4) and the actions (a–d).

1 His girlfriend *b* (on the phone)	a doesn't know the Green Parrot Café.
2 The first woman Sean asks	b arranges to meet Sean at a café.
3 The man he asks	c knows where the café is and shows him part of the route.
4 The second man he asks	d knows where the Blue Moon Café is.

4 Look at the Talk Builder. How do you say the expressions in **bold** in your language?

Talk Builder Directions

A: Excuse me. Do you know the Green Parrot Café? How do you get to it from here?
B: **Cross** the street. **Turn right. Go past** the cinema and then **turn left**.
C: **Go along** the street for about 100 metres. You'll see the station in **front of you**. The Green Parrot is next to it.

➡ SKILLS BUILDER 41

---

5 **3.28** Pronunciation Listen and repeat the questions.

6 Use the map on page 119 to choose the correct directions from A to the Orange Kangaroo Café.

Turn left. Go along the street for about 50 metres. Go past a ¹*cinema/church* and then go past a ²*restaurant/shop*. You'll see a ³*church/station* in front of you. Turn left and go along the street for 300 metres. Go past a ⁴*park/two cafés* and you'll see the café on the right.

7 Speaking Work in pairs. Ask for and give directions from one of the places (A, B or C) to different cafés on the map.

8 Work in pairs. Ask for and give directions in your town.

➡ SKILLS BUILDER 41

1 Choose a small area in the centre of your town or city. Make a list of six places in it. Use the ideas (a-e) to help you.

a a famous square
b a cinema or theatre
c a sports stadium
d a restaurant or café
e a disco

2 ➡ SKILLS BUILDER 42 Look at the strategies for asking for and checking directions.

3 Work in pairs. Choose one of the places in your town. Take turns to ask for and give directions to different places from it.

9 Where did you give directions to? Tell the class.

I gave Anna directions to a new café.

Writing Workshop 5

1 Look at the photos (a–c) on the postcard. What country is it from?

2 Read the postcard and check your guess from Exercise 1. Find the names of the places in the photos (a–c).

Hi Graham,
I am now in Buenos Aires. It's a fantastic city and it's got some beautiful buildings. Last night, we went to a club to see a tango show and have dinner. It was great! Before Buenos Aires we were in Patagonia and went to the Perito Moreno Glacier. We also visited the Valdes Peninsula to see the whales and penguins. Tomorrow, we're going north to visit the Iguazu Falls. I love it here because Argentinian people are really friendly. Yesterday, I bought a book to learn Spanish.
Hasta la vista! (see you soon)
Charlie

Text Builder

3 Order the information (a–e) in Charlie's postcard.

a Where he is going tomorrow.
b Where he is now and a description. *1*
c What he did last night.
d Why he likes the place.
e Where he went before and what he did.

4 Look at the Sentence Builder. What word(s) do you use in your language to express purpose?

Sentence Builder *to* for purpose

1 We went to a club **to** see a tango show and have dinner.
2 We also visited the Valdes Peninsula **to** see the whales and penguins.
3 I bought a book **to** learn Spanish.

→ SKILLS BUILDER 26

---

5 Use cues and the linker *to* to write sentences.

1 this afternoon / I / am going / to the beach / go surfing
This afternoon, I am going to the beach to go surfing.
2 she / bought / camera / take photos of animals
3 we / went / to the national park / see the turtles
4 they / visited / London / go shopping
5 I / got up / at six o'clock / finish my homework
6 he / bought / postcards / send to his family

6 Write a postcard to a friend.

→ SKILLS BUILDER 27

1 Choose a place: a country or a region of your country. Imagine you are on a tour and make notes about the things in Exercise 3.

2 Use your notes to write the postcard.

3 Check your answer for mistakes.

7 Work in groups. Read your partners' postcards. Which is the most interesting tour? Tell the class.

10 GADGETS

Objectives: Listen, read and **talk about** technology; **act out** shopping situations; **write** a notice; **learn about** the Present Perfect.

a

b

TOPIC TALK

1 Which of the gadgets in the network can you see in the photos (a-c)? Check your answers on page 117. Which of them would you like to have?

a *It's probably a USB flash drive.*

2 3.29 **3.30** Listen to three people (1-3). What are their favourite gadgets and what new gadgets would they like to have?

1 *Her favourite gadget - a tablet*

3 3.31 **3.32** Listen again to the first person. Complete the information in the network.

My gadgets

I am ¹*into/not into* technology.
I often ² _____ and I ³ _____ .
My favourite gadget is a/an ⁴ _____ .
I like it because it's so ⁵*cool/useful.*
I'd like to have a new ⁶ _____ .

4 3.33 **Pronunciation** Listen and write down the words. Then <u>underline</u> the main stress.

Flash drive

LANGUAGE CHOICE 67: VOCABULARY PRACTICE

5 Work in groups. Use the network to tell your partners about *your* use of technology. How many people in the group are really into technology?

Online

buy things online, check/send emails/messages, download music/films/photos/programs, go online, play online computer games, read articles and blogs, upload photos/information, use Facebook/Skype

Gadgets

digital camera, DVD player, e-book reader, mobile phone, MP3 player, Sat Nav, smart phone, TV, USB flash drive, video camera, video game console

Computers

desktop, laptop, net book, tablet

c

28 GRAMMAR
USELESS GADGETS?

Warm Up

1 Look at the gadgets in the photos (a-d) and match them with their functions (1-4).

1 you put your money here *a*
2 you get directions from this
3 you read books on this
4 you put your phone or MP3 player on this

2 Read the opinions (1-3) in the forum. Who writes about gadgets that:

a are unnecessary?
b have a negative influence on people?
c have some useful features?

3 Do you agree with the opinions from the text? Why/Why not?

Present Perfect

4 Look at the irregular verbs list on page 95 and the 3rd forms of verbs in blue in the text. Match them with the infinitives below.

regular verbs: a use - _used_
b stop - _____ c learn - _____
d want - _____
irregular verbs: e buy - _____
f spend - _____ g have - _____

5 Read the sentences below and find more examples of the words in bold in the text. Then complete the rule.

Affirmative
have/has + 3rd form of the verb
I/We/You/They **have learned** a lot about e-book readers.
She/He **has spent** a lot of money on them.
Negative
haven't/hasn't + 3rd form of the verb
I/We/You/They **haven't used** an e-book reader.
She/He **hasn't tried** any of her gadgets.

• We use the Present Perfect when we *want to say/don't want to say* exactly when something happened in the past.

ABOUT US   FAVOURITES   TOP TEN   NEWS   GOS

Gadget Zone!

What are your opinions on gadgets?
Write your comments here!

1 I haven't used an e-book reader but my friend has got one and I have learned a lot about them. She's got an e-book reader and she loves it. It's small so she can put it in her pocket and it's got a lot of books in it. The only problem is that you can't read in the bath!
Linda, 21, Leeds

2 A lot of gadgets are expensive and not very useful. My mother has bought a lot of new travel gadgets like a mobile phone hammock and 'safe sandals'. She has spent a lot of money on them. It's funny because she doesn't travel a lot so she hasn't used any of them.
Pete, 17, Manchester

Practice

6 Complete the sentences with the verbs in brackets in the Present Perfect.

1 I _have had_ (have) six mobile phones in my life.
2 I _____ (sell) my old computer and
   I _____ (buy) a new laptop.
3 I _____ (not use) an e-book reader but
   I _____ (use) a Mac.
4 I _____ (read) a lot about net books but
   I _____ (not hear) anything about tablets.

→ LANGUAGE CHOICE 68

7 Read the Sentence Builder. Translate the sentences (1–2) into your language. Where do we put *never* (a or b)?

a between *have* and the 3rd form of the verb
b at the beginning or end of the sentence

Sentence Builder *never*

1 I have **never** had a car with a Sat Nav.
2 I have **never** wanted a Sat Nav.

3 People are less intelligent and creative because of gadgets – they have stopped using their brains. I always use paper maps and I have never wanted a Sat Nav. I've never had a car with a Sat Nav and I'm not going to buy one. They are often wrong and sometimes dangerous because you have to look at the screen when you are driving.
Chris, 53, Brighton

8 Complete the sentences with *never* and the correct forms of the verbs in the Present Perfect.

1 My sister _has never had_ a smart phone. (never / have)
2 I _____ a laptop. (never / use)
3 We _____ travel gadgets. (never / buy)
4 My friends _____ here. (never / be)
5 I _____ an email from my mobile. (never / send)
6 My father _____ a computer game. (never / play)

→ LANGUAGE CHOICE 69

9 Use the cues to make sentences in the Present Perfect.

1 My teachers / upload our homework / never
   My teachers have never uploaded our homework.
2 I / buy a lot of books online
3 My girlfriend / not hear / about net books
4 We / try a lot of online games
5 My mother / not download a film / never
6 My granddad / surf the internet / never

Grammar Alive
Talking about achievements

10 [3.35] Listen to the dialogue. What are Sandy's and Jamie's achievements?

Jamie has won a competition.

11 Work in pairs. Use the cues to make dialogues.

A: *I have put my photos online.*
B: *I've never put my photos online but I've uploaded my essays.*

A starts	B answers
1 put my photos online	1 upload my essays
2 write a blog	2 read a lot of blogs
3 made a video	3 take a lot of photos

B starts	A answers
4 play in a rock band	4 learn to play the guitar
5 win an online competition	5 win an essay contest
6 write a song	6 write a story

12 Write three sentences about your achievements. Share them with a partner.

29 INTERNET ADDICTS

Warm Up

1 Work in pairs. Look at page 118 and ask and answer the questions in the quiz. Is your partner an internet addict?

Reading

2 Read the article quickly. Match the headings (a–e) with the paragraphs (1–4). There is one extra heading.

a Suggestions for internet use
b Good things about the internet
c Kevin's internet use *1*
d Janet and Jonathan's internet use
e Problems of internet use

3 → SKILLS BUILDER 14 Use the strategies in the Skills Builder to match the sentences (a–f) with the gaps in the article (1–5). There is one extra sentence.

a Between five and ten percent of users have problems because of their internet use.
b She sometimes forgets to do things because she is busy on Facebook.
c Because of that he does not concentrate and has problems at work. *1*
d Once, he arrived late for work because of this.
e Go out with friends and join clubs to meet new people.
f Because of that, he is often tired and has problems at school.

4 Do you agree about the dangers of internet use and the suggestions in the article? Tell the class your opinions.

Some people use it too much but normal use is okay.

5 Vocabulary Look at the Word Builder. How do you say the words in **bold** in your language?

Word Builder *have*

1 He is **having** breakfast.
2 He **has** problems at school.
3 His friends **have** parties.
4 You can **have** fun online.

→ LANGUAGE CHOICE 70: VOCABULARY PRACTICE

Technology

Nowadays, we spend hours online but is it good for us? *Sally Evans* investigates.

3.36

1 Kevin McDonald checks his emails when he is having breakfast. He uses his smart phone on the train to work and gets nervous in tunnels where there is no internet connection. At his office, he uses two computers and his phone and checks his messages every minute. ¹_c_ In the evening, he plays computer games and goes to sleep with his net book on the bed. When the family are on holiday, Kevin uses his smart phone to check his emails on the beach.

2 Kevin's wife, Janet, does not like his internet use but she spends four hours online every day, too. ²_____ Their son, Jonathan, has got two computers in his bedroom and plays online computer games, sends messages and does his homework at the same time until late at night. ³_____ He sometimes stays at home and plays games on the computer when his friends have parties.

6 Work in pairs. Ask and answer the questions.

1 Do you ever use your mobile or computer when you are having breakfast?
2 Do you check messages on your mobile when you are out having fun with friends?
3 Do you ever have problems at school because of your mobile?
4 How often do you have parties? How do you invite your friends to them (by email, by text)?

Writing

7 Read the notice. Why is the phone important for Alice?

Lost Smart Phone
Yesterday, I lost my new smart phone near the school science laboratory. It is a black Lokia XJ834Z and is very small (9 cm x 5 cm).

My grandma gave me the phone for my birthday last week. Also my old phone has no internet connection!!!!!!
If you find it, please contact the school secretary and give her the phone.

Alice Colman (Year 10)

⊘ SKILLS BUILDER 28

8 Look at the Sentence Builder. How do you say the sentences in your language?

Sentence Builder Indirect object

1 My grandma gave **me** the phone. (My grandma gave the phone to me).
2 Give **her** the phone. (Give the phone to her.)

↘ LANGUAGE CHOICE 71

9 Put the words in the correct order to make sentences.

1 digital camera / gave / My dad / me / a new
   My dad gave me a new digital camera.
2 an / me / send / Please / email
3 me / a question / Ask
4 a letter / Let's / write / her
5 about the party / a message / sent / I / her

Psychologists think some people are ʼnternet addicts'. ⁴_____ Some experts also ʼink 'normal' use causes concentration ʼroblems and stress. People also have more ʼnline friends than in the real world.

If you are worried about your internet ʼse, count the hours you spend online and ʼduce them. Take a break every hour when ʼou are online. ⁵_____ The internet is useful ʼd you can have ʼn online but it ʼn be bad for ʼou, too.

10 Choose one of your favourite things (e.g. a smart phone, a tablet computer). Write a 'lost' notice for the school notice board. Include this information:

- where at school you lost it
- a description of the object (colour/make/size)
- why it is important for you
- who to contact

11 Work in groups. Read your partners' notices. Try to guess the person.

This is Monika's notice because it is her mobile.

Your Choice

No Comment

'They call it "surfing the net". It's not surfing. It's typing in your bedroom.'

Jack Dee, British comedian

GRAMMAR
PET GADGETS

Warm Up

1 Look at the photo. What is happening? Is the dog happy?

2 Read the interview. Which of these gadgets has Charlie designed?

a a dog shower
b a life jacket for cats
c dog sunglasses

Present Perfect: questions

3 Read the questions from the interview and complete the pattern below.

> **Questions**
> **Have** you/we/they **tested** it on a dog?
> **Has** anyone/he/she **bought** it?
> What other gadgets **have** you/we/they **invented**?
>
> **Short answers**
> Yes, I/we/you/they **have**. / No, I/we/you/they **haven't**.
> Yes, he/she **has**. /
> No, he/she **hasn't**.

- (What) + _____ / _____ + subject + 3rd form of the verb

4 Use the cues to write questions about Charlie Liu.

1 What gadgets / he / invent?
   What gadgets has he invented?
2 people / buy / his gadgets?
3 his gadgets / become popular?
4 he / make a lot of money?
5 What gadgets / his dog / test?
6 he / design a mobile phone for dogs?

➤ LANGUAGE CHOICE 72

5 Read the Sentence Builder. Translate *ever* into your language.

> **Sentence Builder** *ever*
> 1 Has your gadget **ever** won a competition?
> 2 Have you **ever** designed a gadget for cats?

(3.37)

We are at the Pet Gadget Show in Los Angeles. We're talking to a famous inventor, Charlie Liu. Charlie has designed a lot of pet gadgets.

Reporter: This box is a dog shower. Have you tested it on a real dog?
Charlie Liu: Yes, I have. My dog loves it!
R: Has anyone bought it?
CL: No, but a lot of people have asked about it.
R: What other gadgets have you invented?
CL: Oh, a lot. I have invented a life jacket for a dog. And my partner has designed dog sunglasses.
R: You've done a lot of work for dogs! Have your gadgets ever won a competition?
CL: Oh, yes, my dog mobile phone won last year.
R: Have you ever designed a gadget for cats?
CL: No, I haven't. I've never designed anything for other animals. I love dogs!

6 Use the cues to write questions in the Present Perfect with *ever*. Then ask and answer the questions in pairs.

1 you / design a gadget?
A: *Have you ever designed a gadget?*
B: *No, I haven't.*

2 your best friend / buy you a gadget?
3 your friends / upload photos?
4 you / test gadgets?
5 your grandfather / use a smart phone?
6 your teachers / send you emails?

Grammar Alive
Talking about experiences

7 **3.38** Listen to the dialogue. What gadget shows has Chris been to?

8 Work in pairs. Use the cues to ask and answer questions.

A: *Have you ever used a tablet?*
B: *No, I haven't, but I've used a net book.*

A starts	B answers
1 use a tablet?	1 use a net book
2 be abroad?	2 travel a lot in my country
3 write a story?	3 read a lot of stories

B starts	A answers
4 read a science fiction book?	4 watch some science fiction films
5 sell anything?	5 buy a lot of things
6 see a gadget show?	6 see some art exhibitions

Speaking Workshop 10

1 Vocabulary **Work in pairs. Look at the vocabulary box below. What features are important for you when you choose a mobile phone?**

A: *For me, the design and colour are important.*

Mobile phone features
design/colour, GPS (navigation system),
internet connection, long battery life,
radio and MP3 player, memory (e.g. 70 gigabytes),
touch screen (big/small screen), video camera (e.g. 5.0 megapixels), video phone

2 3.39 DVD 10 **Listen or watch Listen to or watch the dialogue. Answer these questions.**

1 What features of the first phone does the customer not understand?
2 Why does he decide not to buy the second phone?
3 What features has the third phone got? Why does the customer buy it?
4 Why is the shop assistant unhappy when the customer leaves?

3 3.39 DVD 10 → SKILLS BUILDER 6 **Listen and watch Listen to or watch the dialogue again. Is the dialogue formal or informal? Use the strategies on page 106 to help you.**

4 **Look at the Talk Builder. Which of the sentences do the shop assistant (SA) and the customer (C) say?**

Talk Builder Shopping

1 **Good morning, sir/madam. Can I help you?** SA
2 Yes, **I'm looking for** a new mobile phone.
3 **Has it got** a camera?
4 **Is it** easy to use?
5 **How much** is it?
6 **Could you show me** a cheaper one, please?
7 **This one's** thirty-six pounds.
8 **I'd like that one**, please.

→ SKILLS BUILDER 43

5 3.40 Pronunciation **Listen and repeat the sentences from the Talk Builder.**

6 **Use the Talk Builder to complete the dialogue below.**

A: Good morning, sir. ¹ *Can* I help you?
B: Yes, I'm looking ²_____ a digital camera.
A: This is an Olympik XZ 55.
B: How ³_____ is it?
A: It's two hundred and fifty pounds.
B: ⁴_____ you show me something cheaper, please?
A: This ⁵_____ is only eighty pounds.
B: I'd ⁶_____ that one, please.

7 Speaking **Work in pairs. Act out the dialogue in Exercise 6. Take turns to buy a mobile.**

8 **Work in pairs. Act out a shopping dialogue.**

→ SKILLS BUILDER 43

1 **Work in pairs. List the features of a mobile phone or a different gadget.**

Mobile phone: camera (10 megapixels), memory – 30 GB, MP3 player

2 → SKILLS BUILDER 44 **Look at the strategies for describing objects when you do not know the words.**

3 **Work in pairs. Use your notes and the strategies to act out a shopping situation. Take turns to be the shop assistant and customer.**

9 **What kind of phone did you 'buy' from your partner? Tell the class.**

I bought a fantastic phone with a great camera and a very big memory.

Language Review Modules 9 and 10

❶ My country/Travel/ Nationalities/Gadgets/*have* Choose the correct words to complete the texts.

I am ¹*Turkish/Turkey* but I live in ²*German/Germany*. We live in a small town near the ³*capital/centre* city, Berlin. The ⁴*season/weather* here is nice in the ⁵*spring/national parks* and summer but the winters are cold and ⁶*hot/snowy*. At weekends, I often go hiking in the ⁷*lake/mountains*. I can get there by ⁸*plane/car*. On Sundays, we often ⁹*take/have* lunch at a restaurant near our home. We always ¹⁰*make/have* fun because my family is very big and I've got ten cousins and they are my age.
I'm ¹¹*into/in* technology so I've got a lot of modern gadgets like an e-book ¹²*player/reader* and a smart phone. I ¹³*download/use* music and films and I buy things ¹⁴*online/blogs*. I've got a ¹⁵*digital/desktop* computer but I usually use my net book.   */15*

❷ *to* for purpose Combine the sentences into one.

16 I came here. (I want to get some information.)
17 We bought a dictionary. (We wanted to learn more words.)
18 She is taking her laptop. (She wants to work on the train.)
19 They went to Greece. (They wanted to do some sightseeing.)   */4*

❸ Indirect objects Order the words in the sentences.

20 grandmother / My / presents / me / buys / expensive
21 camera / give / your / Don't / her / new
22 her / I / my / lend / sometimes / computer
23 gave / I / interesting / him / an / book   */4*

❹ *a/an/the* Complete the text with *a, the* or -.

I am ²⁴_____ student at ²⁵_____ university. I live in ²⁶_____ small flat and go to classes by ²⁷_____ bus. ²⁸_____ classes are very interesting. There are ²⁹_____ students from around ³⁰_____ world here.   */7*

❺ Indefinite pronouns Complete the sentences with *someone, anyone, everyone, no one*, etc.

31 All the people have left. There's _____ here.
32 What are you looking for? I can't see _____ interesting in this shop.
33 This café is too expensive for us. _____ is more than £5.
34 Let's go to India! I'd like to go _____ interesting.
35 We have to leave the train. Look, _____ is leaving!   */5*

❻ Present Perfect/*never, ever* Use the cues to write sentences in the Present Perfect.

36 I / have / a lot of accidents
37 My grandfather / never / be / abroad
38 you / ever / buy / an expensive gadget?
39 My dog / never / eat / fruit
40 We / not spend / a lot of money on gadgets
41 your class / win / a competition?
42 Our teachers / travel a lot   */7*

❼ Directions Complete the text with the words *cross, turn, past* or *along*.

If you want to get to the police station, you have to go ⁴³_____ this street for 200 metres. Then ⁴⁴_____ this street, go ⁴⁵_____ the post office and ⁴⁶_____ left. You'll see the police station in front of you.   */4*

❽ Shopping Complete the gaps in the dialogue (47–50) with the phrases (a–e). There is one extra phrase.

a Has it got a good battery?
b Yes, I'm looking for a net book.
c I'd like that one, please.
d Has it got a camera?
e How much is it?

A: Good morning. Can I help you?
B: ⁴⁷_____
A: This is a new NOTE net book.
B: ⁴⁸_____
A: Yes, it has.
B: ⁴⁹_____
A: Yes, you can work for about eight hours.
B: ⁵⁰_____
A: It's £300.   */4*

Self Assessment

3.41 Listen and check your answers.
Write down your scores. Use the table to find practice exercises.

Exercise	If you need practice, go to
1	Language Choice 61, 64, 65, 67, 70
2	SB p.86 ex 4
3	Language Choice 71
4	Language Choice 62, 63
5	Language Choice 66
6	Language Choice 68, 69, 72
7	SB p.85 ex 4
8	SB p.93 ex 4

LEARNING LINKS: 1 Read and listen to the article about telephone songs in Culture Choice 5 on page 105.
Then do a project about the use of phones.
2 Exam Choice 5 → My Lab / Workbook pages 108–109.
3 Check Your Progress 10 → MyLab / Workbook page 110. Complete the Module Diary.

IRREGULAR VERBS

Infinitive	2nd form (Past Simple)	3rd Form (Past Participle)
be	was/were	been
become	became	become
begin	began	begun
break	broke	broken
bring	brought	brought
build	built	built
burn	burned/burnt	burned/burnt
buy	bought	bought
catch	caught	caught
choose	chose	chosen
come	came	come
cost	cost	cost
cut	cut	cut
dig	dug	dug
do	did	done
draw	drew	drawn
dream	dreamed/dreamt	dreamed/dreamt
drink	drank	drunk
drive	drove	driven
eat	ate	eaten
fall	fell	fallen
feed	fed	fed
feel	felt	felt
fight	fought	fought
find	found	found
fly	flew	flown
forget	forgot	forgotten
forgive	forgave	forgiven
get	got	got
give	gave	given
go	went	gone
grow	grew	grown
have	had	had
hear	heard	heard
hide	hid	hidden
hit	hit	hit
hold	held	held
hurt	hurt	hurt
keep	kept	kept
know	knew	known
lead	led	led
learn	learned/learnt	learned/learnt
leave	left	left

Infinitive	2nd form (Past Simple)	3rd Form (Past Participle)
lend	lent	lent
let	let	let
lie	lay	lain
light	lit	lit
lose	lost	lost
make	made	made
mean	meant	meant
meet	met	met
pay	paid	paid
put	put	put
read	read	read
ride	rode	ridden
ring	rang	rung
run	ran	run
say	said	said
see	saw	seen
sell	sold	sold
send	sent	sent
set	set	set
shine	shone	shone
show	showed	shown
shut	shut	shut
sing	sang	sung
sit	sat	sat
sleep	slept	slept
smell	smelled/smelt	smelled/smelt
speak	spoke	spoken
spend	spent	spent
spill	spilled/spilt	spilled/spilt
stand	stood	stood
steal	stole	stolen
swim	swam	swum
take	took	taken
teach	taught	taught
tear	tore	torn
tell	told	told
think	thought	thought
throw	threw	thrown
understand	understood	understood
wake	woke	woken
wear	wore	worn
win	won	won
write	wrote	written

Culture Choice 1

1 Look at the photos (a-c). Read the sentences (1-5). Guess which sentence is false?

1 New York City has eight million people.
2 There are about forty thousand homeless people (people with no home).
3 Ninety-five percent of homeless people sleep in shelters (simple hotels with bedrooms and bathrooms).
4 Sixty percent of New Yorkers are Hispanics (from Latin America).
5 New Yorkers speak 138 different languages.

2 4.1 4.2 Listen to two interviews with New Yorkers. Check your guess from Exercise 1.

3 4.1 4.2 Listen again. Choose the best answer to these questions.

1 Where does Tom usually sleep when it's not cold?
  a streets or parks   b shelters
  c the subway (the New York Metro)
2 How does he get money?
  a he works with tourists   b he plays the guitar
  c he works in a park
3 What does he like about New York?
  a it's an easy city   b it's a big city   c it's his city
4 Where does Miriam live?
  a in Manhattan   b near an airport
  c in the centre of New York
5 How many people live in her house?
  a 4   b 5   c 6
6 What does she like about her city?
  a the people   b the languages   c the culture

4 Your Culture Work in pairs. Ask and answer the questions about *your* home town or city.

1 How many different languages do people speak?
2 Are there a lot of homeless people?
3 Where is your home? (e.g. near the centre)
4 What do you like about your city or town?

5 Read the information about O. Henry on page 97. What are his stories about?

6 4.3 Read and listen to the short story. Order the events (a-g).

a Soapy goes to a restaurant but he can't get in.
b Soapy sings and dances in the street.
c Soapy decides to work and rent a flat.
d The police put Soapy in prison.
e It starts to be cold in New York. 1
f Soapy breaks a shop window with a bottle.
g Soapy takes a man's pen.

7 Read the story again. Match the sentences (1-5) with the reasons (a-e).

1 Soapy usually goes to prison in December *e*
2 Soapy does bad things
3 The man in the office doesn't call the police
4 Soapy goes to prison
5 Soapy plans to get a job

a because he is homeless.
b because he wants to change his life.
c because he wants to go to prison.
d because he has problems with them.
e because he gets cold in New York.

My Culture Project

8 Write notes about your home.

• where it is: in a village/town/city
• the rooms in your home
• the things in it
• your bedroom

9 Use your notes to write a description of your home. Include two false things.

10 Read your partner's descriptions. Can you guess the false information?

O. Henry (1862-1910)
American writer of short stories
Real name: William Sydney Porter
Jobs: farm worker, bank worker, journalist, writer
Family: married with one daughter
Problems: three years in prison (money problems at the bank); problems with alcohol
His stories: funny stories about everyday life in the USA

Soapy hasn't got a home and lives on the streets of New York. He likes the sun and trees and doesn't like houses or jobs. For nine months of the year, Soapy is a happy man. Then the first week of December comes and it gets very cold. Soapy has the same plan every December – to do a bad thing and go to prison for three months.

First, Soapy visits an expensive restaurant and wants to have a big lunch and then say 'Sorry, I haven't got any money.' But when Soapy walks into Sanborn's Restaurant the waiter says, 'You can't come in here. Sorry.'

Soapy thinks of a new plan. He goes to an expensive shop and takes a bottle. He hits the window with the bottle. A policeman comes but at that moment he sees a man running away from the shop. No prison for Soapy this afternoon.

That evening, Soapy goes to a street with a lot of theatres. Rich men and women in expensive clothes are going into the theatres. Soapy starts to sing and dance and talk to the people. There is a policeman but he says to the people: 'He's a student from a theatre school. Don't worry about him.'

Soapy is angry and unhappy. How can he get into prison for the winter? He sees a man in an office and goes in and takes his pen.

The man goes after him. 'Stop! That's my pen.'
'Call the police then,' says Soapy.
But the man doesn't call the police because he has problems with them.
'Okay, maybe it is your pen,' he says to Soapy.

Soapy sits down and makes a new plan. Maybe he can get a job and some money. Then he can get an apartment and some good clothes. Maybe he is too old for the street. Tomorrow he decides to find a job.

Then Soapy hears a person next to him. 'Excuse me,' a policeman says. 'What are you doing here? What's your address? Where do you work?'
'I haven't got a home but I want to get a job tomorrow,' says Soapy.
'No address. Come with me. Three months in prison for you,' the policeman says.

Culture Choice 2

1 What childhood memories have you got of animals?

My grandmother had a big, black cat called Twining.

2 Match the animals (1–5) with the pictures (a–e).

1 tortoise   4 pigeon
2 seagull   5 scorpion
3 snake

3 4.4 4.5 Listen to a description of Gerald Durrell's life in Corfu. Are the sentences true (T) or false (F)?

1 Gerald had two sisters and a brother. *F*
2 He went with his family to Corfu in 1935.
3 Quasimodo was a female pigeon.
4 Leslie was angry because there were snakes in the bath.
5 The family returned to England in 1949.
6 Gerald worked in a zoo when he left school.
7 Gerald died in 2005.

4 4.6 Use the glossary to read and listen to an extract from *My Family and Other Animals*. Choose the best summary (a–c).

a The Durrell family have a quiet lunch at home.
b Gerald's animals scare the family.
c Gerald's scorpions bite Lugaretzia.

5 Read the text again and order the events (a–h).

a The scorpion and her babies got onto the dining-room table.
b Gerald found a scorpion and her babies in the garden. *1*
c Gerald took the scorpions to the garden.
d Roger the dog bit Lugaretzia on the leg.
e Gerald put the scorpions into a matchbox.
f The family left the room and Gerald found the scorpions.
g The family were very scared and wanted to kill the scorpion.
h After lunch, Larry opened the matchbox and saw the scorpions.

6 Work in pairs. Ask and answer these questions.

1 What animals in Exercise 2 are you scared of?
2 What animals do you like?
3 Have you got animals at home? What animals?
4 Did you collect animals when you were younger? What animals?

My Culture Project

7 Choose a famous person from your country. Find out information about his/her early life and write notes about these things:

- the person's name – why he/she is famous
- when he/she was born – his/her family
- early life – e.g. school/university
- when he/she became famous
- what he/she did in his/her life (e.g. wrote books about …)
- when he/she died

8 Work in pairs. Tell your partner about your person.

My Family and Other Animals

Gerald and his family moved into a new villa with a big garden. An old man worked in the garden and his wife, Lugaretzia, helped in the house. There were always a lot of Larry's friends – writers and painters – in the house and Gerald had a lot of time to look for new animals.

One day, I found a female scorpion with a lot of little babies on her back. I was excited by this new family and I decided to take them to my bedroom. I put them carefully into a matchbox and went to the villa. Lunch was ready, so I left the matchbox on the table in the sitting-room and went into the dining-room for a meal.

Larry finished eating and went to find his cigarettes. I watched him when he opened the matchbox. With her babies still on her back, the female scorpion climbed out and walked on to Larry's hand.

Larry felt a movement and looked down. Then he screamed. Lugaretzia dropped a plate and Roger ran out from under the table. Larry shook his hand and the scorpion landed on the table between Margo and Leslie. The babies went everywhere. The scorpion was angry and ran towards Leslie. He jumped up, knocked his chair over and the scorpion ran towards Margo. She screamed. While Mother put on her glasses to see what the problem was, Margo threw a glass of water over the scorpion. The water hit Mother. Now the scorpion was under Leslie's plate and the babies were everywhere.

'It's that boy again!' shouted Larry.

'Be careful. They're coming!' screamed Margo.

'We need a book,' cried Leslie. 'Hit them with a book!'

'What's happening?' asked Mother.

'One's coming towards me.'

Roger thought that we were in danger. Since Lugaretzia was the only stranger in the room, he bit her on the leg.

When everyone was a little calmer again, all the babies were under the plates, knives and spoons. The family left the room and I found the scorpions and took them to the garden.

1 Look at the photos (a-e) from Tim Burton's film, *Alice in Wonderland*. Do you know the film or book? Do you like it? Do you know any more children's stories or films that are popular with adults?

2 `4.7` `4.8` Listen to descriptions of five characters from Wonderland (1-5). Match them with the photos (a-e).

3 `4.7` `4.8` Listen again. Match the personality adjectives (1-4) with the characters in the photos (a-e).

1 polite and friendly
2 very nervous and worried about the time
3 not very polite and talkative (x 2) *a*
4 intelligent and relaxed

4 Read about Lewis Carroll on page 101. Match the answers (a-e) with the questions (1-5).

1	Who did Lewis Carroll tell stories to? *e*	a	the changes a child experiences when he/she becomes older
2	What happens in the stories?	b	that life is more complicated than she thought
3	What is the book about?	c	Alice visits a strange world and has adventures
4	What does Alice learn in Wonderland?	d	children and adults
5	Who are the stories popular with?	e	the children of a friend

5 `4.9` Use the glossary to read and listen to the extract from *Alice in Wonderland*. Are the sentences true (T) or false (F)?

1 The characters are happy to see Alice. *F*
2 The Hatter and the Hare are not very polite to her.
3 The Hatter had problems with his watch.
4 His watch shows the date and the year.
5 For the Hatter it is always the same day.
6 Alice doesn't understand the Hatter.

6 Match the two parts of the sentences about the situation. Which is the strangest thing?

1	They say there are no places at the table but *d*	a	there isn't any.
2	They offer Alice some wine but	b	they don't wash them.
3	The Hare repaired the Hatter's watch but	c	it doesn't tell the time.
4	The Hatter has got a watch but	d	there are a lot of them.
5	The teacups are dirty but	e	he used butter and it doesn't work.

My Culture Project

7 Choose a character from your country's literature. Write notes about these things:

- appearance: physical appearance/clothes
- personality
- what he/she does in the story

8 Work in groups. Tell your partners about your character.

My favourite character is Captain Nemo from Jules Verne's Twenty-thousand Leagues Under the Sea. He is ...

A Mad Tea Party

There was a big table with a lot of chairs round it. But there were only three at the table: the Mad Hatter, the March Hare and a large brown mouse. The Mouse sat between the Mad Hatter and the March Hare. It was asleep, so they talked over its head.

When they saw Alice, they cried, 'No, no, you can't sit here! There isn't a place for you!'

'There are lots of places,' Alice said. She sat down in a chair at one end of the table.

'Have some wine,' the Mad Hatter said politely.

Alice looked round the table but there was only tea.

'I don't see any wine,' she answered.

'There isn't any,' said the March Hare.

'Then why did you say, 'Have some wine'? It wasn't very polite of you,' Alice said angrily.

'We didn't invite you to tea but you came. That wasn't very polite of you,' said the March Hare.

The Mad Hatter opened his eyes very wide but he didn't speak. Then he took out his watch and looked at it. 'What day is it?' he asked. Alice thought for a little. 'Wednesday, I think,' she said.

'My watch says Monday,' the Mad Hatter said. 'You see I was right. Butter isn't good for a watch.' He looked angrily at the March Hare.

'But it was the best butter,' answered the March Hare.

'Yes, but you put it in with the bread knife. Perhaps some bread got in.' The March Hare took the watch from the Mad Hatter and looked at it sadly. Then he put it in his tea. He took it out and looked at it again. Alice looked at the watch. 'It's a strange watch!' she said. 'It tells you the day but it doesn't tell you the time.'

'So? Does your watch tell you the year?!' asked the Mad Hatter.

'No,' Alice answered, 'but it's the same year for a very long time.'

'And my watch doesn't tell the time because it's always tea-time.'

Alice thought about that. 'I don't really understand you,' she said politely. She looked around the table. There were a lot of teacups on the table.

'We move from place to place,' said the Mad Hatter.

'Don't you wash the cups?' asked Alice.

'No, we don't have the time,' said the Mad Hatter.

'Why not?' asked Alice.

'It's a long story,' said the Mad Hatter. 'Time was my friend, you see. But he and I aren't friends now. So he doesn't help me and now I have no time.'

'I see,' said Alice and smiled politely. But she didn't really understand.

Lewis Carroll (real name Charles Dodgson) wrote *Alice in Wonderland* in 1865. Carroll was a young teacher at Oxford University; he did not have a family but he was good friends with the Liddell family and their four young children. He told the children stories about a girl's adventures in a strange world – Wonderland. The stories were about the change from the simple life of a child to the more complicated world of an adult. First, Alice can't get into Wonderland because she is very big so she drinks and eats things to change her size. Then she also meets a lot of strange people and has a lot of problems. When Carroll published the stories, they were very successful and are now famous around the world. Lewis Carroll's stories are for children but are also popular with adults. One of the most recent film versions was Tim Burton's 2010 *Alice in Wonderland*.

Glossary
angrily: (adv) in an angry way
mad: (adj) mentally ill
polite: (adj) to behave correctly

a b c d

1 Work in pairs. Look at the photos (a-d) and ask and answer the questions.

1 Which of the chocolate in the photos would you like to eat or drink?
2 How popular is chocolate in your country? What are the most popular kinds of chocolate or chocolate dishes?
3 How much chocolate do you eat every week? What is your favourite kind of chocolate?

2 4.10 **4.11** Listen to the radio programme about chocolate. In what order does the expert mention the things in the photos (a-d)?

1 - d

3 4.10 **4.11** Listen again and choose the best answers to these questions.

1 Where do people eat the most chocolate?
   a Belgium   b the USA   c Switzerland
2 Where did people first start making chocolate?
   a Europe   b Mexico   c the USA
3 Who started to drink chocolate with sugar in it?
   a the Aztecs   b the Spanish   c the Swiss
4 Where did Daniel Peter start to mix milk and chocolate?
   a Belgium   b Britain   c Switzerland
5 What is good for you to eat every day?
   a a lot of milk chocolate
   b 100 grams of dark chocolate
   c white chocolate

4 Read the information about Joanne Harris on page 103. What is important in her books? Why?

5 4.12 Read and listen to the film review *Chocolat*. Order the information (a-d) in the review.

a opinions about the film
b the beginning of the film
c basic information about the film
d what happens in the film

6 Read the review again and answer these questions.

1 Why can't the villagers eat the chocolates?
2 Why do they go to Vianne's shop?
3 Why does the mayor get angry?
4 How is Vianne a kind person?
5 What character is Johnny Depp in the film?
6 What is not so good about the film?
7 What are the good things about the film?
8 Why are the chocolates the stars of the film?

7 Would you like to watch the film or read the book? Why/Why not?

My Culture Project

8 Write notes about a film from *your* country. Include this information:

- basic information: title/year/the director/the actors
- what happens in the story (not the end of the film)
- why it is good or bad

9 Work in groups. Take turns to ask and answer these questions about your film.

1 Who is the director?
2 Who are the main actors?
3 What happens at the beginning of the film?
4 What happens next?
5 Who are the main characters?
6 What are the best things about the film?
7 What is not so good about the film?

CHOCOLAT

In 1959, Vianne Rocher (Juliette Binoche) and her young daughter move into a small French village and Vianne opens a chocolate shop. It is the period before Easter when people can't eat things like meat and sweets but some villagers start to go to Vianne's shop because her chocolates are so good.

The local mayor, Comte de Reynaud (Alfred Molina), is very angry. For him, the chocolate shop is a temptation for the villagers and he does not like Vianne because she does not go to church. Gradually, more people start to come to the shop and try Vianne's delicious chocolates. She is a fantastic cook, she knows the best type of chocolate for every person and she helps people in the village with problems. Vianne also meets a good-looking Irish traveller, Roux (Johnny Depp), and falls in love with him. With Roux's help, she organises a big chocolate festival on Easter Sunday.

The story of the film *Chocolat* comes from the novel by Joanne Harris and the director is Lasse Hallström. The main actors are Juliette Binoche (Vianne Rocher) and Alfred Molina (Comte de Reynaud); Johnny Depp and Judi Dench are also in the film.

The story is interesting but very predictable. It is also strange because it happens in a French village where the people speak English! One of the best things about this film is the great acting; Juliette Binoche and Alfred Molina are fantastic. There are also some good dialogues and the photography is amazing, too. Because the photography is so good, the real stars of the film are the chocolates – when you are watching it you want to eat them and when you leave the cinema you feel hungry!

Joanne Harris (1964 -) is from the north of England but her mother is French. She studied languages at Cambridge University and was a teacher for fifteen years after she left university. Her third novel, *Chocolat*, is about a chocolate shop in France - it was a bestseller and became a film in 2001. Food is always a theme in her books. When she was young, Joanne's grandparents had a sweet shop and she wrote a cookery book, *My French Kitchen*, in 2002.

Glossary
delicious: (adj) food that is very good
Easter: (n) a Christian festival (March/April)
fall in love: (v) to start to be in love with a person
mayor: (n) someone who is the head of the government in a town, city or village
predictable: (adj) when you know what is going to happen
temptation: (n) when you want something badly
villager: (n) a person who lives in a village

1 Your Culture **Look at the photos (a-c). Answer the questions below for people in your country.**

1 When do people answer calls on their mobile phone?
   a when they are at home
   b in lessons or work meetings
   c on public transport
   d when with friends in a café

2 How do people answer their mobile phone in public places?
   a they answer quietly
   b they are very noisy
   c they talk about private things
   d they move away from other people

3 What is the most popular use of mobile phones?
   a talking
   b sending text messages
   c playing games
   d taking photos

4 What are the rules for mobile use in schools?
   a no mobiles in the school
   b no mobiles on in class
   c you can use mobiles in breaks
   d you can use mobiles all the time

2 **Discuss the answers to the questions in Exercise 1 with the rest of the class.**

3 4.13 **4.14** **Listen to a radio documentary about mobile phones and cultural differences. Are the sentences true (T) or false (F)?**

1 It is usually rude to answer the phone in public in Japan. *T*
2 In Sweden, people talk loudly on their mobiles.
3 Japanese people text more than they talk on their mobiles.
4 Americans like very small, smart phones.
5 In Britain, people decorate their phones with stickers.
6 You can use a mobile in class in most British and American schools.

4 4.13 **4.14** **Listen again. Which countries mentioned are similar to your country in mobile phone use?**

5 4.15 **Read and listen to the information about telephone songs and the artists. Answer the questions.**

1 What problems does the man in the first song have?
2 Who does he talk to first?
3 Where did Stevie Wonder's song do well?
4 What type of music is it?
5 Why does the woman in Lady Gaga's song not answer the phone?

6 4.16 **Read and listen to the song lyrics by Stevie Wonder and answer the question. Use the glossary to help you.**

Why is he calling?

a it is a very special day
b he is in love with her
c the weather is very good
d he sees something beautiful

7 4.16 **Listen and read again. Match the words in blue in the song (1-4) with the drawings (a-d).**

Telephone Songs

The first telephone song appeared in 1899 and was called *Hello my Baby*. In the song, a man phones his girlfriend every morning to talk to her. But first he has to speak to the operator and he has to talk very loudly because the line is so bad. Phone calls appeared in a lot of pop songs in the 20th century, like Stevie Wonder's *I Just Called to Say I Love You* in 1984. The famous American soul singer's song was number one in countries, like the USA, Britain, Germany and Italy and won an Oscar for best original song in 1985.

In the last few years, phone songs have been about mobile phone calls. The most famous is Lady Gaga's *Telephone*. A woman is dancing at a club when her boyfriend calls. 'I can't hear you and I'm busy,' she says. The boyfriend rings again and again but the woman doesn't answer because she is dancing and having fun.

What will pop songs be about in the future? There will probably be more songs about social networking, like *New Friend Request* by Gym Class Heroes. But they will still be about love!

I Just Called to Say I Love You

No New Year's Day to celebrate
No [1]chocolate covered candy hearts to give away
No first of spring
No song to sing
In fact here's just another ordinary day.

No April rain
No [2]flowers bloom
No wedding Saturday within the month of June
But what it is, is something true
Made up of these three words that I must say to you.

Chorus
I just called to say I love you
I just called to say how much I care
I just called to say I love you
And I mean it from the bottom of my heart.

No summer's high
No warm July
No [3]harvest moon to light
one tender August night
No autumn breeze
No [4]falling leaves
Not even time for birds to fly to southern skies.

No Libra sun
No Halloween
No giving thanks to all the Christmas joy you bring
But what it is, though old so new
To fill your heart like no three words could ever do.

Glossary
bottom: (n) the lowest part of something
breeze: (n) soft wind
bring: (v) to have something with you when you go somewhere
care: (v) how you feel when someone is important for you
celebrate: (v) do something special
fill: (v) to put a lot into something
give away: (v) to give to people
heart: (n) an organ – you need it to live
high: (n) happy moment
joy: (n) when you are happy
light: (v) to make a place light
must: (v) to have to
though: (conj) but
warm: (adj) quite hot
within: (prep) in

My Culture Project

8 **Work in pairs. Think of five questions to ask about people's use of phones. Give options.**

Do you answer your mobile when you're on a bus or train?
a *sometimes*   b *never*   c *always*   d *occasionally*

9 **Work in groups. Ask and answer your questions. Tell your class about the answers.**

Three people in the group usually answer their phones on buses or trains. Two people ...

🎧 Listening

1 Getting the general idea of dialogues (multiple choice)
Page 21, Exercise 1

- Before you listen, look at any photos with the exercise. What can you see in them? Think about these things:
  Where is the situation (e.g. a shop/a club/a school)?
  Who are the people (e.g. family/friends)?
- Make a list of the things that you can see in the photo (e.g. canoes). Write down the words.
- Then read the exercise. Check the meaning of the words. Try to guess the answer to the exercise.
- Listen to or watch the dialogue and check your guess. Do not try to understand all of the words.

2 Getting specific information (text completion)
Page 35, Exercise 7

- Look at the exercise. Try to guess the kind of information you need to complete the gaps. For example, is it a time, a number, a day, a date, a sport?
- Listen the first time to get the general idea. Answer some of the questions.
- Listen again and try to answer all the questions.
- Be careful with times and numbers (e.g. sixteen and sixty).
- When you don't know the answer, make a guess!

3 A focus on context (matching)
Page 51, Exercise 6

- Look at the list of situations. Underline the place (e.g. on the phone) and the people (friends).
- When you listen, use sounds (e.g. telephone sounds) to help you guess the place.
- Listen for words about the situations (e.g. dancing/dance = party).
- Think about the people in the dialogues. Who are they (e.g. brother/sister/friends)? Is it their first meeting?
- Use expressions to help you (e.g. *My name's …* , *Hi there, Jamie.*)
- Choose a situation for each dialogue.

4 Identifying the topic of part of a text (matching)
Page 66, Exercise 2

- Look at the list of things to match (e.g. topics and questions). Underline important words (e.g. types of films).
- When you listen, do not try to understand every word. Listen for words related to the topics (e.g. *types of films = old black and white films*).

5 Identifying intentions (matching)
Page 83, Exercise 9

- Look at the list of intentions of the speakers.
- Think of language for the different intentions: Ask for information - *What time … ?* Suggest - *Let's …* Requests - *Can you … ?* Ask for permission - *Can I … ?*
- Listen the first time to get the general idea of the situation. Who is speaking (e.g. Lucy to her brother/friend?)? Where are they?
- Listen again. Listen for the language (e.g. *Can you … ?*) for different intentions. Also get the general idea about what the people want. Notice the speakers' tone of voice.

6 Identify formal style
Page 93, Exercise 3

- You can identify formal style in dialogues from this language (informal examples in brackets):
a **Saying hello**
  Good morning/Good afternoon. (Hi/Hello)
b **Titles**
  Sir/Madam - used by a shop assistant/waiter, etc.
c **Requests**
  Could you (Can you) show me something cheaper, please?

Reading

7 Getting the general idea (multiple choice)
Page 18, Exercise 2

- First, look at the text. When there are titles and headings in the text, read them.
- Look at photos and maps with the text. What are they about?
- Read the question and check the meaning of new words. Can you guess the answer from the photos and titles?
- Now read the text quickly and check your guess. Do not try to understand all of the words.

8 Identify informal style (matching)
Page 22, Exercise 3

- Personal letters, emails and notes are usually informal:

  starting letters etc.: *Hi; Hi there; Hello; How are you?*

  finishing: *Write soon; See you; All the best; Love*

  punctuation: contractions (e.g. *can't*); *AMAZING* (capital letters); *!!!!!!!* (exclamation marks); – (dashes); *xxxxx* (kisses at the end of a letter)

9 Getting the idea of parts of a text (matching)
Page 42, Exercise 2

- Read the text first to get the general idea. Then look at any headings there are. Check the meaning of new words.
- Read every paragraph carefully, especially the first sentence. It usually introduces the topic of the paragraph.
- Underline important words in the paragraph. Then choose a heading for the paragraph or write down the topic of the paragraph.

10 A focus on context (matching)
Page 50, Exercise 2

- Before you read, look at the design of the texts. Are they from a website, newspaper or notice board? Look for these things: hypertext and links (website); picture and basic information (poster); small letters, special print (newspaper).
- Read the text and answer these questions. Who is it for (e.g. local people or an international audience)? Is it to sell a product or a service?
- Decide on the type of text from the list.

11 Getting specific information (multiple choice)
Page 58, Exercise 4

- Read the text quickly to get the general idea.
- Check the meanings of new words. Make guesses about the answers.
- Read the text again. Underline the parts of it with information about the questions.
- Read that part carefully and choose an answer (e.g. true/false, a/b/c/d) or write the answer.

12 Identifying intentions (multiple choice)
Page 66, Exercise 7

- Look at the list of intentions. Underline important words (e.g. the history). Think of the type of information for them: e.g. history – when it started/who started it.
- Read the text and identify information in it from the list of intentions (e.g. c - clothes/tickets). Then choose the one with the most information.

13 Guessing meanings of new words (matching)
Page 74, Exercise 3

- Find the words in the text and underline the sentences they are in. Answer these questions: What is the word: a verb, adjective, noun or adverb? (e.g. roof = noun)
- Are there any words that are similar to words in your language? Is the meaning similar?
- Does the type of text (an article about food) or the sentence (e.g. about fresh food) help you to guess the meaning?
- If you can't guess the meaning of a word, use a dictionary to help you.

14 Identifying connections (sentence gaps)
Page 90, Exercise 3

- Read the text to get the general idea. Identify the paragraph topics (e.g. 1 = Kevin's internet use).
- Read the sentences to match with the gaps and identify the topics (e.g. a = internet addiction). Underline linking words (e.g. because of).
- Read the sentences before and after the gaps. Underline pronouns (e.g. he/she) and verbs (e.g. take a break (imperative)).
- Choose sentences for every gap. Check that it fits the sentences before or after it.

Writing

15 Linkers: *and/or*
Page 22, Exercise 4

and for lists:
*I study history, maths **and** French.*

and to describe two actions
*I read books **and** do my homework.*

or to describe alternatives:
*I play tennis **or** basketball.*
*I play computer games **or** do my homework.*

16 Personal letter
Page 22, Exercise 6

> KEY
> informal style
> linkers

Hi Sandra,

introduction

A How are you and your family? We're fine here in Los Angeles and I really like the lifestyle.

life in a new city

B Los Angeles is a big city but it's different from London and it's very relaxed. We've got a house with a swimming pool and it's twenty minutes from the beach by car. At the weekend, I go swimming and surfing. Surfing is difficult but it's great fun!

life at school

C I go to Santa Monica High School – it's a big school but the people are very friendly. It's hard work and I've got eight classes every day. In the afternoon, I play football ('soccer' here) or basketball. When I get back home, I have a swim or do my homework – yes we have TWO HOURS of homework! Then I watch TV and go to bed early.

ending

D Is it cold and horrible in London? It usually is in February !!!!!!!!

Write soon.
All the best,
Christine

17 A description of a house (prepositions of place)
Page 27, Exercise 7

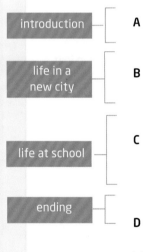

My house is very modern. In my bedroom, I've got a stereo system and a TV. There is a TV in the shower so I can watch my favourite programme. In the kitchen there is an intelligent fridge. There is always food in it because it orders food automatically. On the kitchen table there is an automatic coffee maker. In the living room, I've got an exercise bike with a computer and there is a home cinema on the wall. The home computer is in the hall – I can phone it when I'm not at home. I can check the house when I am at work or at the cinema.

18 Linkers: *and/but*
page 38, Exercise 3

and to add information
*It is in the zoo club **and** it starts at nine o'clock.*

*The music is good **and** the people are friendly.*

but to contrast information
*It is a great club **but** it is expensive.*

*The people are friendly **but** the music is not very good.*

19 Short notes and replies
Page 38, Exercise 5

A suggestion to go out

a Hi Chloe,
What are you up to at the weekend? Do you fancy going to the cinema on Saturday night? There's a good new film with Emma Watson and Robert Pattinson. It starts at eight o'clock and tickets are £7. Why don't we meet at my place at seven?
Ring me.
Georgina

Reply - a different suggestion

b Hi there,
Thanks for the invitation. I want to see that film but I've got a better idea. There's a teen night at that new club (Igloo). Why don't we go? It starts at 9.00 on Saturday and tickets are ten pounds. It's got live rap music (Dr Faustus) and a really good DJ!
Chloe

Reply - agree/make arrangements

c Hi,
Okay, that's a great idea! I love dancing but the clubs in this town aren't for teenagers. Let's meet at my place at seven and my dad can take us there and collect us.
See you on Saturday.
G

20 A memory (time linkers)
Page 43, Exercise 7

It was 2 February and it was very cold. I was on a bus when this very attractive girl got on. She sat down and then started to read a book. Then she looked at me and asked, 'Do you know this town? I am new here.' She had a very nice smile.
I helped her and then we had a coffee. After we left the café, she gave me her number. We met at the weekend and then went to the cinema. Before the film, we had a pizza and talked. We forgot about the film!

21 Linkers: *because/so*
Page 54, Exercise 3

because to explain reasons
*I can't play basketball **because** I am tired.*
*I can't come on Saturday **because** it's my dad's birthday.*

so to explain results
*I'm tired **so** I can't play basketball.*
*It's my dad's birthday **so** I can't come on Saturday.*

22 Invitation notes and replies
Page 54, Exercise 5

An invitation to a party

a Hi there,
It's my birthday on Friday so I'm having a small party. We're having lunch and then we're playing table tennis in the afternoon because I got a new table from my grandmother.
Would you like to come?
Please text or call me. See you.
Tom

Reply - can't come

b Hi there Tom,
Thanks for the invitation. I'd like to come but I can't because I'm busy on Friday. My uncle from Canada is here so we're going to London.
Thanks anyway,
Lucy

Reply - accept/information

c Hi Tom,
Thanks for your invitation. I'd love to come to the lunch! I'm sorry but I can't play table tennis in the afternoon because I'm going to a concert with my girlfriend.
See you on Friday.
Cheers,
Oliver

Writing

23 Giving information about people
Page 59, Exercise 7

Tom is a student at Manchester University. He is a person with a very sociable personality and is very friendly. He is interested in football and he is a player in the university team.

24 A formal email
Page 70 Exercise 6

KEY
formal style
addition linkers

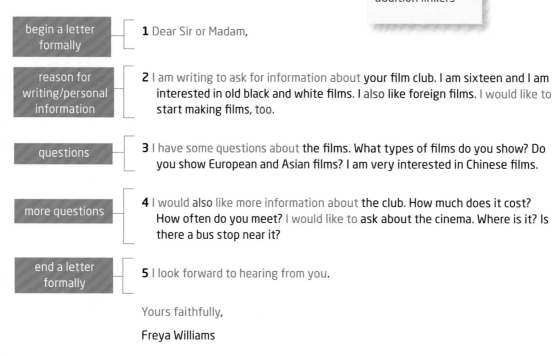

| begin a letter formally | **1** Dear Sir or Madam, |

reason for writing/personal information — **2** I am writing to ask for information about your film club. I am sixteen and I am interested in old black and white films. I also like foreign films. I would like to start making films, too.

questions — **3** I have some questions about the films. What types of films do you show? Do you show European and Asian films? I am very interested in Chinese films.

more questions — **4** I would also like more information about the club. How much does it cost? How often do you meet? I would like to ask about the cinema. Where is it? Is there a bus stop near it?

end a letter formally — **5** I look forward to hearing from you.

Yours faithfully,

Freya Williams

25 Linkers: *because/because of*
Page 75, Exercise 6

- We use *because* and *because of* to explain reasons:

because of + noun
I don't like that hotel **because of** the food.
I didn't have lunch **because of** the time.

because + noun/pronoun + verb
I don't like that hotel **because** the food there is not very good.
I didn't have lunch **because** I didn't have time.

26 Linker: *to*
Page 86, Exercise 4

to for purpose

*We are going to London **to** see a concert.*
*I bought a book **to** read on the train.*

*I go to the park in the afternoon **to** meet my friends.*
*I want to meet Tom **to** talk about that history project.*

27 A postcard
Page 86, Exercise 6

KEY
informal style
to for purpose

where she is now

what she did last night

Hi Sam,

I am now in London. It's a fantastic city and it's got some beautiful buildings. Last night, we went to the Albert Hall to see a concert. It was fantastic! Before London, we were in Scotland for a few days and we went to St Andrews to play golf. Tomorrow, we're going to Oxford to meet my cousin – he's studying there at the university. I love it here because I can practise my English. Yesterday, I bought some English books to read at home.

See you soon,
Monika

where she went before

where she's going tomorrow

why she likes the place

28 Lost property notice
Page 91, Exercise 7

KEY
indirect objects

title

description

why important

Lost Net Book

Yesterday, I lost my new net book near the school library. It is a black Gamgumg X79 and is not very big.

My dad gave me the net book for Christmas. Also my old computer is very slow.

If you find it, *please* contact the school secretary and give her the net book.

Tom Barker (Year 11)

where?

contact

🗨 Speaking

Classroom Language

A Asking about spelling
Page 7, Exercise 14

A: **Can you spell** your name, please?
B: T-H-O-M-A-S
A: **Can you spell** *address*?
B: A-D-D-R-E-S-S

B Asking for repetition
Page 8, Exercise 7

A: I don't understand. Can you repeat that, please?
B: Sorry, can you play the CD again, please?

C Asking for meaning
Page 9, Exercise 7

A: **What's** *notebook* **in** French?
B: *Cahier.*
A: **What's** *caballo* **in** English?
B: *Horse.*

D Asking to use things
Page 11, Exercise 13

A: **Can I use** your pencil, please?
B: **Sorry**. I need it.
C: Of course, you can. Here you are.

E Asking about homework
Page 13, Exercise 10

Student: Have we got homework?
Teacher: Yes, you have.
Student: What is it?
Teacher: Do Exercise 6 on page twenty-one.
Student: When's it for?
Teacher: For Friday.

F Asking for permission
Page 14, Exercise 7

Student: **Can** I go to the toilet, please?
Teacher: **Of course you can**.
Student: **Can** I close the window, please?
Teacher: **Sorry, you can't.**

29 Meeting people
Page 21, Exercise 3

Meet a person you know
A: **Good morning**, Katy, **how are you**?
B: I'm fine thanks.
Introductions
A: **This is** my friend, Lucy.
B: **This is** Tom.
Meet a new person
A: **Hello**, Lucy. **My name's** Tom.
B: **Hi there**. **Nice to meet you**.
A: **Hi there**.
B: **Hi, good to meet you**.
Say goodbye
A: **See you later**!
B: **Bye**, Katy! **Have a good time**!
A: **And you**.

30 Preparation (strategies)
Page 21, Exercise 7

- Before you do a role-play in class, practise phrases from the Talk Builder. Use the model dialogues in the Skills Builder (e.g. Skills Builder 29).
- Say the phrases out loud (e.g. *My name's Javier. Nice to meet you*)
- Underline phrases with difficult pronunciation. When you have problems, ask your teacher to help you.
- Use the MyEnglishLab to practise new phrases at home.

31 Suggestions
Page 29, Exercise 4

A: Mm, I'm thirsty.
B: **Why don't you** look in the fridge?
A: **Good idea**. I'm bored. There's no internet and I can't go on Facebook.
B: **Why don't you** watch TV?
A: **All right**. But this TV's no good.
B: **Why don't you** read a book?
A: **No**, I'm tired. **Let's** go shopping.
B: **I'm not sure**. There are only three shops in this town. **Let's** play a game of chess.
A: **No**, I don't want to. You always win. **Let's** play Monopoly!
B: **Okay**.

32 Understanding people (strategies)
Page 37, Exercise 7

- When you don't hear a person very well or don't understand, ask them to repeat:
  I'm sorry. Can you repeat that, please?
- Repeat the information to check it.

A: *The concert's at eight thirty.*
B: *Eight thirty?*
A: *Yes, it's in the sports centre.*
B: *The sports centre?*
A: *Yes, the sports centre in Cowley.*
B: *Cowley?*
A: *Yes, you can get the number 39 bus there.*
B: *The 39 bus?*
A: *That's right. It goes from the post office.*
B: *The post office?*
A: *Yes, the post office in Broad street.*
B: *Broad street?*
A: *Yes!*

33 Asking for information
Page 37, Exercise 4

A: **Can we have some information about** concerts for this weekend, please?
B: **Of course**. There's a Lady Gaga concert on Saturday.
A: **How much** are the tickets?
B: Tickets **cost** from fifty to a hundred pounds.
A: **What other** concerts are there?
B: There's a concert on Sunday with a London group.
A: **What kind of** music do they play?
B: Rock.
A: **Where** is the concert?
B: At Zoco in North London.
A: **What time** does it start?
B: At eight thirty.
A: **Can I have** two tickets, please?
B: **Of course**.

34 Talking about memories
Page 45, Exercise 4

A: **Do you remember** when we went to that party?
B: Oh, yes. **I remember** that.
A: **And** before the party we went to the shops. It was a great party.
B: Yes, the party was brilliant.
A: **Do you remember** that very tall boy?
B: **I don't remember** his name. He was very nice and he was a good dancer.
A: **I don't remember** that.
B: **You don't remember because** you were with Susan. You danced and then you went into the garden. **And after that** you went home.

35 Listening actively (strategies)
Page 45, Exercise 6

- When you listen to a person, show interest: Use gestures and facial expressions.

Say these words:
Yes. Right. Okay.
- Use questions to show interest:
  Yes? Really?

Speaking

36 Requests
Page 53, Exercise 3

A: Can you lend me your dictionary, please? Mine is very old.
B: Sure, no problem.

A: Could you lend me a pencil, please? I left mine at home.
B: I'm sorry, I can't because this is my only pencil.

A: Could you help me with this reading? I don't understand these words.
B: Sorry, I've got a lot of homework.

37 Describing people in photos
Page 61, Exercise 4

A: This is a photo of me and my friends.
B: Which one's your girlfriend?
A: Sally's the one **on the left** in the red dress. She's standing **at the front.**
B: Which of the boys is your friend Max?
A: He's standing **next to** me. He's the one in jeans and a green T-shirt.
B: Who are those guys **at the back?**
A: The one **in the middle** with short hair is Tom.
B: And who is the guy in the green shirt **on the left.** Tim?
A: Yes, that's Tim. He's a friend from school. And the girl **in the middle** is Pat.

38 Hesitation (strategies)
Page 61, Exercise 7

- When you are speaking (e.g. describing a person) you need time to think.
- In English, you can use these sounds to hesitate:
  Mm, Er ...
- You can also use these words:
  Well, *he's got red hair.*
  She's from Brazil, **you know**.

39 Agreeing and disagreeing
Page 69, Exercise 3

Likes and dislikes

Affirmative
A: I love watching action films.
B: Me too.

Negative
A: I don't like romantic comedies.
B: Me neither.

Opinions

1 Agree
A: It's a fantastic film.
B: That's true.

2 Disagree
A: She's a great actress.
B: I don't like her.
A: That film is boring.
B: I don't agree.

40 At a café
Page 77, Exercise 4

Waiter: Hello, **can I help you?**
Customer 1: What have you got for lunch?
Waiter: Here's the menu. I'm sorry there's no pizza.
Customer 2: Thanks.
Waiter: What would you like?
Customer 2: I'd like a big cheeseburger, **please.**
Customer 1: For me, a lasagne, **please.**
Waiter: What would you like to drink?
Customer 1: An orange juice **for me, please.**
Customer 2: A small bottle of water **for me, please.**
Customer 1: How much is that?
Waiter: That's twelve pounds twenty.
Customer 1: Here you are.
Waiter: Thanks.

41 Asking for and giving directions
Page 85, Exercise 4

A: **Excuse me**? I don't know London and I'm a bit lost. **How do you get to** Trafalgar Square **from here**?

B: **Trafalgar Square?**

A: Yes.

B: Well, **cross this street and turn left**.

A: **Can you repeat that, please?**

B: **Cross this street and turn left**.

A: Okay.

B: **Go past** the church and **then turn right**.

A: Okay, **cross this street**. **Go along** the street and **turn left**.

B: No, **turn right**. Then **go along the street for about 200 metres**. **You'll see** Trafalgar Square **in front of you**.

A: Right, **go along** the street and I'll see it **in front of me**.

B: Yes, that's right.

A: Great, thanks.

42 Asking for and checking directions (strategies)
Page 85, Exercise 8

- It is a good idea to have a map to help you.
- First get the person's attention:
  Excuse me?
- When a person asks for directions, repeat words to check meaning.

A: How do you get to the London Eye?
B: **The London Eye?**
A: Yes.

- When the person is giving directions, ask him/her to repeat when necessary.

A: Cross this street. Go past the theatre and turn right.
B: Sorry, can you repeat that?

- Check directions. Most people can only remember two or three.

A: Okay, cross this street. Go along the street and turn right.
B: **Cross this street, go along the street and turn right?**

43 Shopping
Page 93, Exercise 4

A: Good morning, sir. **Can I help you?**

B: Yes, **I'm looking for** a new mobile phone.

A: This is the latest model. It's a Lemon xphone 7SG.

B: **Has it got** a camera?

A: It's got an MP3, GPS, FM radio and *two* 10 megapixel cameras.

B: What does that mean exactly?

A: It means you can listen to music or the radio.

B: **Is it easy to use?**

A: **Yes, it is**. It's got a touch screen and it's big, too. You can watch films on it and make video calls, too.

B: **How much is it?**

A: **It costs** five hundred and twenty pounds.

B: Have you got anything cheaper? **How much is that phone?**

A: It's sixty-five pounds.

B: Okay. **I'd like that one**, **please**.

A: Would you like to pay by card or cash?

B: Cash, please. Here you are. Sixty-five pounds.

A: Thank you very much.

44 Describing objects (strategies)
Page 93, Exercise 8

- When you don't know (or you forget) a word in English, don't stop speaking! Do one of these things:
- Try to make a word in your language English. (e.g. calculadora = calculador - English word = calculator.
- A lot of words with initials are the same in different languages (e.g. GPS, MP3, FM). Say them with English pronunciation. (GPS - gee, pee, es).
- Use gestures and sounds to describe a word: (e.g. camera)

PAIRWORK, SCORES AND RESULTS

Get Ready, Lesson B, Exercise 6

Read out the instructions to your group:

Look at the teacher.
Don't look at (name of student).
Open your coursebook on page twenty-five.
Look at the photos.
Read the text.
Write a sentence about your favourite star.
Tell your partner about your favourite star.
Open your Students' Book on page fifty-five.
Open your notebook.
Write two new words in it.
Close your books.

M1, Speaking Workshop, Exercise 7

Take turns to act out the dialogues below.

A: *Good morning, Tina. How are you?*
B: *Fine thanks.*

1 Meet a person you know

Student A: the manager of the club (Lucy/Luke)
Student B: a member of a club (Tina/Tim)

2 Introductions/meet a new person

Student B: the member of a club (Tina/Tim)
Student C: the new member of the club (Karen/Chris)
Student A: the manager of the club (Lucy/Luke)

3 Questions about personal information (age, address, abilities)

Student A: the manager of the club (Lucy/Luke)
Student C: the new member of the club (Karen/Chris)

4 Say goodbye

Student A: the manager of the club (Lucy/Luke)
Student B: the member of a club (Tina/Tim)
Student C: the new member of the club (Karen/Chris)

M5, Topic Talk, Exercise 1

Beach volleyball is similar to indoor volleyball. It started in California in 1920 and it became an Olympic sport in 1996. The best teams are Brazil, the USA, Germany and China.
Ice hockey started in Montreal in Canada in 1875 and is similar to hockey. It became an Olympic sport in 1924 and is popular in countries like Canada, the USA, the Czech Republic and Russia. It is a very fast and dangerous sport.
Yoga started in India in about 2000 BC. Yoga is not a sport but it is now very popular in the West and is very relaxing.

M5, Lesson 15, Exercise 1

ARE YOU A FITNESS FREAK?

1 **How many types of exercise do you do regularly (running, swimming, cycling, aerobics, tennis, judo, etc.)?**
   a three or more – 4 points
   b one or two – 2 points
   c none – 0 points

2 **How often do you exercise?**
   a five times a week or more – 4 points
   b regularly once or twice a week – 2 points
   c sometimes – 0 points

3 **Do you wear special clothes for different sports, e.g. cycling or aerobics?**
   a I wear different clothes for every sport. – 4 points
   b I've got one or two sets of sports clothes. – 2 points
   c I do exercise in my old clothes. – 0 points

4 **How do you feel after exercise?**
   a Great! I want to do more. – 4 points
   b Tired but good. – 2 points
   c I want to go to sleep. – 0 points

Results:
0 – 4 points – You are not into exercise.
Try to exercise more often and more regularly.
6 – 10 points – You like sport but you are not a fitness freak.
12 – 16 points – You are a fitness freak!

M6, Lesson 16, Exercise 1

Quiz answers

1 The adult brain weighs about _____ .
   a 900g **b** 1600g **c** 1350g
2 The brain has _____ of neurons and brain connections.
   a thousands **b** millions **c** billions
3 The brain uses _____ of our body's energy.
   a 20% **b** 5% **c** 15%

M6, Lesson 18, Exercise 1

1 **How old was the oldest person in history?**
   Jeanne Calment (1875-1997, 122 years, 164 days): the oldest person in history whose age has been verified by modern documentation.
2 **Who lives longer - men or women?**
   Women
3 **How long did people live in ancient Rome?**
   Twenty-eight years
4 **Where in the world do people live the longest?**
   Japan
5 **What lives longer than people?**
   Only some animals: e.g. some fish and tortoises. A lot of plants live long, especially trees.
6 **When do people usually start going grey?**
   You can go grey at any time in your life, but grey hair usually starts in our thirties.
7 **Why do babies sleep a lot?**
   Their bodies are changing.
8 **Which part of our memory do old people lose first?**
   The ability to learn new things and process new information.

M9, Lesson 26, Exercise 7

Lionel Messi: Argentina
Maria Sharapova: Russia
Kobe Bryant and Jesse Eisenberg: USA
Sebastian Vettel: Germany
Penelope Cruz: Spain
Shakira: Colombia
JK Rowling: British (Scottish)

M10, Topic Talk, Exercise 1

a Swiss Army flash drive
This useful knife has got a pen, scissors and a USB flash drive with 8 GB of memory.
b Dog/Cat video camera
What does your dog or cat do when it is out? Find out and film your pet's life.
c TV bag
You can watch your favourite TV series on buses and trains or show friends your holiday videos when you are at clubs.

Student A

M7, Lesson 20, Exercise 11

Choose three questions. Think of a question to add.

1 Which city produces the most films?
   a Los Angeles **c** Rome
   b London **d** Bombay
2 What is the most famous US film award?
   a Golden Globe **b** Grammy **c** Emmy **d** Oscar
3 Who was the director of the film *Avatar*?
   a Steven Spielberg **c** James Cameron
   b Peter Jackson **d** Ridley Scott
4 Who is the voice of Woody in the *Toy Story* films?
   a Tom Hanks **c** Johnny Depp
   b Brad Pitt **d** Keanu Reeves
5 What British actor was in romantic comedies like *Notting Hill, Love Actually* and *Four Weddings and a Funeral*?
   a Daniel Craig **c** Ewan McGregor
   b Hugh Grant **d** Anthony Hopkins
6 Which two of these top Hollywood actresses is not American?
   a Angelina Jolie **c** Cameron Diaz
   b Penelope Cruz **d** Keira Knightley

You can choose more than one answer for questions 2, 4 and 5. Check your answers below.

ARE YOU A REAL FILM FAN?

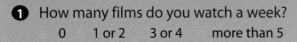

① How many films do you watch a week?

0   1 or 2   3 or 4   more than 5

② What type of films do you like watching?

action films and comedies
films from different countries
old black-and-white films
films by famous directors (e.g. Kubrick/ Hitchcock)

③ How often do you go to the cinema?

never or not very often
3 or 4 times a year
once or twice a month
once or twice a week

④ What do you do when a film is slow and there is no action?

a   leave before the end
b   text friends on your mobile
c   eat popcorn and talk to your friend
d   enjoy the photography, dialogues and acting

⑤ What do you do after a film?

a   leave the cinema and not think about it again
b   go to a café and discuss the film with a friend
c   find out about the film online
d   write about it on your blog

Questions 1 and 3:

a 0 points   **b** 1 point   **c** 2 points   **d** 3 points

Questions 2 and 5:

a 0 points
1 point for answers b-d

Question 4:

Minus 1 point for answers a–c
2 points for answer d

Scores:

0 - 4 points - you are not very interested in films and the cinema
5 - 9 points - you are interested in films but you are not a film fan
More than 10 points - you are a real film fan!

Check your results below.

Are you an Internet addict?

1 How long do you spend online every day?
a up to thirty minutes
b up to two hours
c more than two hours

2 Do you ever feel nervous when you haven't got your mobile or when you are not online.
a never
b sometimes
c often

3 Do you ever have problems with your homework because you are online a lot?
a never
b sometimes
c often

4 Do you ever only sleep a few hours because you have been online at night?
a never
b sometimes
c often

5 Do you ever stay at home online when you can go out with your friends?
a never
b sometimes
c often

6 Do you ever have arguments with your family about your internet use?
a never
b sometimes
c often

M10, Lesson 29, Exercise 1
Questionnaire results

If most of your answers are a) you are not an internet addict.
If most of your answers are b) you need to be careful.
If most of your answers are c) you are possibly an internet addict. Talk to your friends and family about it or get professional help.

M5, Lesson 13, Exercise 12

Describing a scene

M9, Speaking workshop 9, Exercise 1

Map

Student B

M7, Lesson 20, Exercise 11

Choose three questions. Think of a question to add.

1 What US president was a Hollywood actor?
   a Barack Obama   b Ronald Reagan
   c Bill Clinton   d George Bush

2 Which of these films won most Oscars?
   a the *Twilight* saga   b *Lord of the Rings*
   c the *Bourne* films   d *Toy Story*

3 Who was the director of *The Lord of the Rings* trilogy?
   a Peter Jackson   b Steven Spielberg
   c Ridley Scott   d James Cameron

4 Which one of these films was the American actress, Julia Roberts, not in?
   a *Pretty Woman*   b *Erin Brockovich*
   c *Notting Hill*   d *Shakespeare in Love*

5 What kind of film is Thor?
   a romance   b thriller
   c fantasy   d horror

6 Which film festival gives the Golden Bear for the best film?
   a Cannes   b Venice   c Berlin

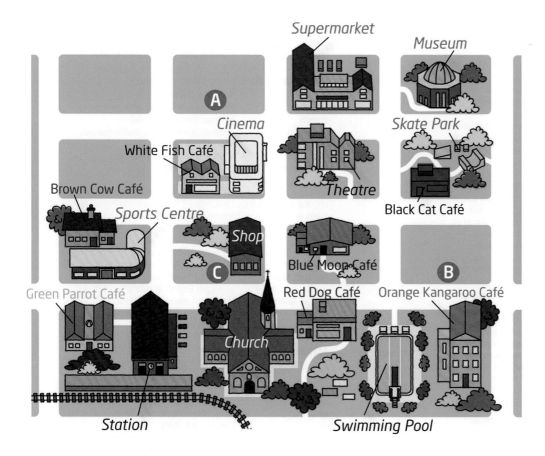

WORD LIST

Get ready B
Page 8   Instructions

complete (v)	Complete the instructions in your book.
listen to	Listen to your teacher.
look at	Look at page 10.
match	Match the words to the photos.
open (v)	Open your dictionary, please.
read	Read the story on page 6.
speak	Speak English in class.
tell	Tell your teacher the answer.
use	Use a pen to write the answer.
watch	Watch the film on TV.
work (v)	Work in pairs to do the exercise.
write	Write in your book.

Get ready C
Page 9   Abilities

count in French	I can count in French.
dance (v)	Can you dance?
download music	You can't download music from the internet.
draw	Mary can draw.
find information	I can find information on the internet.
paint	They can paint pictures.
play an instrument	I can't play an instrument.
play tennis	We can play tennis.
play the piano	Tracy can't play the piano.
play the violin	Pete can play the violin.
play the guitar	Can you play the guitar?
ride a bicycle	He can ride a bicycle.
ride a horse	He can't ride a horse.
say the alphabet	We can say the alphabet.
sing	I can't sing!
ski (v)	Cristina and Mario can ski.
speak Spanish	Sofia can speak Spanish
spell my name	I can spell my name.
swim	Mac can't swim.
tell the time	I can tell the time in English.
upload photos	Can you upload photos on the internet?
write stories	Can you write stories?

Get ready D
Page 10 -11   Objects

bag	The book is in my bag.
book	This is my English book.
CD	Can you play the CD?
computer	Switch on the computer, please.
earring	These earrings are from Brazil.
football	This is my new football.
guitar	That guitar is my dad's.
mobile phone	This is my new mobile phone.
MP3 player	I like your MP3 player.
painting	Those paintings on the wall are fantastic!
photo	This is a photo of my mum.
poster	The poster on the wall is of my favourite band.
scarf	That scarf is from Greece.
shoe	This tennis shoe is mine!
tennis racquet	Use a tennis racquet to play tennis.
T-shirt	My new T-shirt is red and black.

Adjectives

beautiful	Those earrings are beautiful.
cheap	The scarf is cheap.
expensive	My new piano is expensive.
great	This MP3 player is great!
new	My tennis shoes are new and expensive.
old	Dad's shoes are old and cheap.
special	This is my favourite CD. It's special!

Get ready E
Page 12   Family

brother	I've got one brother, Mike.
cousin	My cousin's name is Frank.
dad	My dad's name is Jim.
daughter	My sister is my parent's daughter.
father	Tom's father's name is Mark.
granddad	My father's father is my granddad.
granddaughter	My granddad hasn't got a granddaughter.
grandfather	My grandfather's name is Robert.
grandma	My grandma has got one grandson, Jason.
grandmother	My grandmother's name is Meg.
grandparents	My grandparents are my dad's parents.
grandson	My grandma's grandson is Jason.
husband	Nick's Jane's husband.
mother	My mother's name is Jane.
mum	My mum's name is Jane.
parents	My parent's names are Jane and Nick.
sister	My sister's name is Emmy.
son	My dad has two sons.
wife	Jane is Nick's wife.

Appearance

attractive	Emmy's attractive and she's got a nice smile.
black hair	I've got black hair and brown eyes.
blond hair	Tim's got blond hair.
blue eyes	Helen's got blue eyes.
brown eyes	I've got black hair and brown eyes.
dark hair	Black hair is dark hair.
fair hair	Blond hair is fair hair.
green eyes	Green eyes and blond hair are attractive.
grey eyes	Jane has grey eyes, not blue eyes.
grey hair	My grandma has grey hair.
long hair	I've got long hair, not short hair.
nice smile	Mum's got a really nice smile.
overweight	Dad's a bit overweight now.
red hair	Clare's attractive and she's got red hair.
short	My sister's short, she's not tall.
short hair	You've got short hair, not long hair.
slim	Ruby's slim, she's not overweight.
tall	I'm tall, I'm not short.

Adjectives

friendly	My brother Jack is friendly.
happy	Grandma looks happy in the photo.
hard-working	Dad and Mum are hard-working.
interesting	This book is interesting.
sociable	Emmy is friendly and sociable.
sporty	Clare can play football. She's sporty.

Get ready F
Page 14   School subjects

English	We've got English at quarter past three.
French	We have French every day.
geography	Geography is not my favourite lesson.
history	History is interesting.
information and computer technology (ICT)	ICT is a new lesson.
maths	Maths is my favourite lesson.
physical education (PE)	I'm sporty. PE is my favourite lesson.
science	Science is at five to twelve.
Spanish	Spanish is Tim's favourite subject.

Times

five past one	Spanish is at five past one.
five to twelve	Science is at five to twelve.
half past four	PE is at half past four.
quarter past three	We've got English at quarter past three.
quarter to eleven	Maths is at quarter to eleven.
twelve o'clock	Geography is at twelve o'clock.
twenty to ten	History is at twenty to ten.

Module 1: Lifestyles
Page 15   Free time activities

buy	I buy presents for my wife.
chat	We chatted online for hours.
do	I do sport on Saturdays.
go	We go shopping at the supermarket on Fridays.
go out	I go out on Fridays.
go to	Jenny goes to dance lessons every Monday.
listen to	He listens to music all day.
use	Can I use the internet?

watch	They want to watch a programme on TV.
relax	I relax at home and watch TV.

Interests

computer game	Kids love computer games.
computer	I like computers.
dancing	I like dancing at the disco.
fashion	I'm not interested in fashion.
film	I watch films a lot.
football	I play football in the sports centre.
music	We like this music.
photography	He likes photography.
reading	We like reading!
shopping	I love shopping.
sport	Children play a lot of sport.
swimming	I'm going swimming on Monday.
tennis	I play tennis on Thursdays.
in the morning	I go running in the morning.
on Saturday	I go shopping on Saturday.

Page 16-17   The super-rich

rich	He's very rich; he has a lot of money.
interesting	I think his life is very interesting.
happy	In the photo they look happy.
busy	I can't go out today; I am very busy.
friendly	John is a very friendly person; he likes making friends.
hard-working	They are hard-working students.
bike	I come here by bike.
billionaire	Billionaires are very, very rich!
capital	London is the capital of England.
come from	My mother comes from Canada.
disco	I like the school disco!
hard	I like hard work.
have	We always have fun at the party.
housework	I usually do the housework at weekends.
local	You can get this fruit at your local supermarket.
market	I usually buy fruit and vegetables at the market.
ordinary	Today is a very ordinary day.
private	We have a private swimming pool.
study	She wants to study law at university.
super	They won the lottery. They are super-rich.
teenager	He's a teenager. He's 18 years old.
tired	Small children get tired very quickly.
together	They do the work together.
work	She works in a big office in New York.
over	Over seventy billionaires live in New York.
poor	His family is very poor.
private	I go to private school.
bank	You can change your money into pounds at the bank.
home-cooked	The food in restaurants isn't home-cooked.

Page 17   Adverbs of frequency

always	My dad always loses his car keys.
never	I never read anything.
often	I don't watch television very often.
sometimes	I go there for lunch sometimes.
usually	I usually get up at about 8 o'clock.
horror	I don't like horror films.

Habits

relax	I want to sit down and relax.
start	School starts at 8.30.

Page 18   Report from Australia

area	Camden is my favourite area of London.
bird	There's a bird in the garden.
camel	People ride camels in the desert.
desert	The desert is hot and dry.
kangaroo	Kangaroos on the road are Australian animals.
lizard	Look! A lizard.
second language	Spanish is my second language.
tell	Can you tell me a story?
village	I live in a small village in the country.
Aborigine	Aborigines sometimes live in the Australian desert.
boomerang	Boomerangs come from Australia.
didgeridoo	It isn't easy to play the didgeridoo.
hunt	They hunt animals in this forest.
musical instrument	I can't play a musical instrument like the didgeridoo.
painting	I like the painting of the horse.
traditional	You can read traditional stories in this book.
weapon	The weapon that he used was a knife.
wild	A kangaroo is a wild animal.
artist	An artist paints pictures.

beautiful	Some of the paintings were very beautiful.
clinic	I go to the clinic to see the doctor.
collect	Can you collect all the books and put them on my desk?
follow	I follow her into the house.
have got	We have got time.
lifestyle	He has an interesting lifestyle.
like	People like the Martu have a traditional lifestyle.
meat	I don't eat very much meat.
modern	We use modern farming methods.
share	He shares a room with his brother.
technology	I study modern computer technology.

Page 19   Word builder

bus	I usually catch a bus to college.
child	I am not a child; I'm a teenager!
church	I go to church on Sundays.
family	There are four girls and two boys in my family.
house	We spend Sunday evenings at Harriet's house.
life	Life in the desert is not easy.
party	Fiona invited 25 people to her birthday party.
person	Diana is a very kind person.
story	Dad, can you read me a story?
woman	Maria is a very beautiful woman.

Page 20   Modern life

blog	He writes about his trip in his blog.
online	I go online to check my emails.
student life	Student life is fun but you don't have a lot of money.
the Net	She is online and on the Net all day.
contact	I wanted to get in contact with her but she was on holiday.
help	The internet helps me with my work.
hate	I hate my mobile phones! I never use them.
presentation	I often given presentations to my class.
chat	Let's chat online.

Habits

laugh	The audience always laugh at all the jokes.
phone	How often does Steve phone you?

Page 21   Meeting people

bye	Bye Max! See you on Monday.
fine	"How is Mike?." "He's fine."
good morning	Good morning, class.
hi	Hi John. How are you?
see you later	Bye Cathy! See you later.
habit	Smoking is a very bad habit.
member	I'm a member of the photography club.
personal information	Can you give me your personal information, please?
time	This is my first time in a canoe.
canoe	Bob often goes canoeing.
manager	John is the manager of this hotel.

Module 2: At home

Page 23   Furniture

armchair	Granddad sleeps in the armchair.
bed	It's time to go to bed.
bookshelf	The book is on the bookshelf in the hall.
carpet	I have a thick carpet on the floor of my bedroom.
chair	We have 6 chairs in the kitchen.
cooker	We have a new cooker in the kitchen.
cupboard	The food is in the cupboard in the kitchen.
curtain	Close the curtains.
desk	Put the papers on my desk.
dishwasher	Can you put the plates in the dishwasher after dinner?
door	Close the door, Henry.
floor	He leaves his clothes all over the floor.
fridge	The cheese is in the fridge.
lamp	I use my lamp when I work at night.
microwave	Cook the potatoes in the microwave.
mirror	Anna always looks in the mirror!
oven	Heat the oven to 200 degrees Celsius.
picture	That's a nice picture of Oscar.
plant	She likes to have lots of plants in the house.
poster	My room is covered in posters.
shower	I want a bedroom with a private shower.
sofa	Please sit on the sofa.
stereo system	Put some music on the stereo system.
table	We eat breakfast at the kitchen table.
toilet	The toilet is in the bathroom.
TV	We sometimes watch TV all night.

wall	There is a map of the world on the wall.
wardrobe	Put your clothes in the wardrobe.
washing machine	We wash our clothes in the washing machine.
window	He cleans the windows every week.

My home

comfortable	Are you comfortable sitting on the floor?
favourite	You're my favourite uncle.
flat	There is a new block of flats opposite us.
house	My house has five rooms and a big garden.
light	My room is very light.
tidy	Please leave the house tidy when you go.

Rooms

bathroom	Where is the bathroom?
bedroom	Our house has four bedrooms.
dining room	We eat dinner in the dining room.
hall	You can hang your coat in the hall.
kitchen	Jo is in the kitchen making a sandwich.
living room	I spend the evenings in the living room.
room	This is the room I work in.

Page 24 My room

CD	He's in his room listening to CDs.
dark	It is very dark in this room.
group	He plays the guitar in a rock group.
hobby	My hobbies are playing the guitar and reading.
pet	Do you have any pets?
tarantula	My brother has a tarantula.

Page 25

dictionary	Look it up in a dictionary.
encyclopedia	Do you have an encyclopedia?

Page 26 Smart home

automatically	The camera flashes automatically.
choose	We can choose from lots of films.
cinema	I love going to the cinema.
cold	It's freezing cold outside today.
dinner	They have dinner at 8.
e-book	I love my new e-book.
fruit	Bananas are my favourite fruit.
home	I've got a computer at home.
intelligent	Our intelligent robot understands what we tell it to do.
look after	She looks after her sister's children in the week.
open	Can you open the bag and take the money out?
order	You can phone the restaurant and order the food.
program	We usually program the oven to start at 2 o'clock.
route	This is the route to school.
stay	Do you want to go to Kathy's or stay here?
temperature	The temperature goes down to two degrees at night.
traffic	There isn't a lot of traffic on the roads on Sundays.
vacuum cleaner	Clean the carpet with the vacuum cleaner, please.
warm	Cover the bowl to keep the soup warm.
well	I don't feel very well.

Multi-part verbs (1)

get back	We got back home at 7.
get up	I get up at five a.m. every morning.
go to bed	I'm tired. I want to go to bed.
go to sleep	I went to sleep in the chair.
wake up	Wake up, Sam. Your breakfast is ready.

Page 27 Prepositions of place

in	We live in Poland.
on	My computer is on my desk.
at	Are you at home?
automatic	This is an automatic washing machine.
control	This box controls what I see on the TV screen.
hall	We keep the computer in the hall.
maker	I use a coffee maker every morning.
dream	My dream job is testing computer games!
hi-tech	The new house is very hi-tech and everything is automatic.

Page 28 Micro homes

cup	I have a cup of tea every morning.
electricity	Does your cooker use gas or electricity?
glass	This window is made of glass.
metal	The table is metal with a glass top.
plate	Do you want a plate for your sandwich?
space	We want a kitchen with space for a table and some chairs.

Quantity

notebook	I can't find my notebook.
boy	She is married now and has two boys.
cola	Drinking cola is bad for your teeth.
girl	Lots of girls don't like wearing dresses.
pizza	I want a pizza for dinner.
water	There is a lot of water in the river.
book	The new dictionary is a useful book.
money	Billy always spends lots of money in the shops.
pencil	Can I borrow your pencil?

Page 29 Feelings

angry	My father is angry about the broken window.
bored	Most of the students look bored.
excited	Emma is very excited about the concert.
happy	I'm very happy with the results.
hungry	I'm hungry. What time is lunch?
nervous	Julie is nervous about the test.
sad	Why are you so sad?
scared	My brother is scared of dogs.
thirsty	I'm really thirsty. Let's get a drink.
tired	Young children get tired very quickly.
unhappy	Barbara is unhappy about her exam results.
worried	I'm very worried about my exams.

Suggestions

accept	It is a beautiful gift, but I can't accept it.
all right	"Let's go." "All right, we'll go now."
idea	That's a good idea!
let's	Let's go to the cinema tonight.
reject	"No he doesn't agree. In fact, Mark rejects the idea."
suggest	I suggest that you make a list.
why don't you...?	Why don't you check the numbers again?

Module 3: Downtown

Page 31 Adjectives

boring	This programme is so boring!
busy	It was busy in the city centre today.
cheap	Houses are very cheap there.
comfortable	This is a comfortable bed.
exciting	It is a very exciting game.
expensive	We can't buy this. It's very expensive.
friendly	Everyone in the village is very friendly.
modern	We always stay in a modern hotel.
nice	She's got a nice car.
noisy	I'm live on a noisy city street.
quiet	They live in a quiet little village.
relaxed	She looks happy and relaxed today.

Going out

city	London is the largest city in England.
town	We live in a small town on the coast.

Places

amusement park	We often go to amusement parks on holiday.
art gallery	Let's go to an art gallery at the weekend.
café	Let's have a cup of tea in the café.
cinema	Shall we go to the cinema tonight?
market	I usually buy fruit and vegetables at the market.
museum	There are a lot of things from the past in the museum.
night club	let's go dancing at the night club.
outdoor	We can buy clothes at the outdoor market.
pub	let's meet at the pub for a drink.
restaurant	They have dinner in a Chinese restaurant on Mondays.
shop	The town has some good clothes shops.
shopping centre	We sometimes go to the shopping centre on Saturdays.
skate park	There is a great skate park in London.
sports centre	I play football in the sports centre.
swimming pool	Does the hotel have a swimming pool?
theatre	Let's go to the theatre and see a play.

Page 32 Clubs

alcohol	I never drink alcohol.
DJ	I work as a DJ on the radio.
hip hop	I love hip hop music.
hood	He wears a warm jacket with a hood.
house music	I listen to house music a lot.
jeans	He wears an old pair of jeans.
live	You can see the band live.
rock	I'm in a rock band.
smoking	Smoking is very bad for you.
atmosphere	This restaurant has a really exciting atmosphere.
cool	This is a really cool party!
fantastic	It's a fantastic film!

hamburger	I can't eat that big hamburger!
bad	I had a really bad day.
good	this is a really good club.

Page 33
hot chocolate	I love hot chocolate!
waiter	Where is the waiter?

Page 34 — Free fun
concert	We go to concerts outdoors in the summer.
cinema	There are some good films at the cinema.
game	The game today is between Manchester United and Arsenal.
professional	I want to be a professional football player.
running	Running keeps me fit.
sightseeing	We go sightseeing when we are on holiday.
skating	We all love skating.
street performer	There are fantastic street performers in London.

Verbs and prepositions
come to	Come to London!
go around	We can go around the city all day.
go to	I go to work by train.
listen to	I like listening to all kinds of music.
live in	She lives in London.
look at	Look at that painting!
stay at	He always stays at the Ritz hotel.
walk to	I usually walk to college.
cathedral	There is a beautiful cathedral in the centre of the town.
exercise	Try to do some exercise every day.

Page 34/35 — London for free
acrobat	I'm an acrobat in the circus.
biology	Biology is my favourite subject.
collection	She's got a wonderful collection of books.
cool	He's really cool.
enjoy	The park was lovely. I enjoyed the walk.
exhibition	We often go to exhibitions at the art gallery.
free	Club membership is free.
get	You can get that book at the new bookshop.
interactive	Is this machine interactive?
machine	I wanted to buy some cola from the drinks machine.
musician	He's a fantastic musician.
object	She has several strange objects in her bag.
palace	We went to Buckingham Palace in London.
pop	I don't really like pop music.
square	The police station is in the main square.
store	There's a big furniture store near here.
ticket	How much is a bus ticket to London?
tourist	Tourists spend a lot of money at Portobello Market.
under	Children under five travel free.
visit	We hope to visit Rome in Italy.

Time prepositions
at seven o'clock	The shop closes at seven o'clock.
in the morning	I go to school in the morning.
in the spring	The weather gets warm in the spring.
on Mondays	We have football practice on Mondays.
on Thursday mornings	I stay at home on Thursday mornings.

Page 36 — Skaters
artistic	I'm not very artistic.
build	They want to build a hotel near the beach.
concrete	There are concrete steps to the building.
council	He is a member of the UN Security Council.
experienced	He's a very experienced soldier.
famous	Many famous actors live in Beverly Hills.
graffiti	The school walls are covered with graffiti.
learn	We learned all about dinosaurs in this lesson.
plan	Their plan is to travel around Europe by train.
skater	The park is full of skaters.
spot	This is a great spot for a holiday.
step	There are three steps leading up to the door.
trick	Can you do any skating tricks?
relaxing	I like a relaxing bath after work.
dangerous	Police say the escaped prisoner is a very dangerous man.

Page 37 — Asking for information
cost	The cost of accommodation in the city centre is very high.
of course	"Can I come in?" "Of course, sit down."
kind	What kind of music do you like?
comedy	All my favourite films are comedies.

sell	Do you sell concert tickets?
worried	I'm very worried about my exams.

Page 38
collect	I can collect Jane from the station.
call	I called Sarah at her office in London.
fancy	Do you fancy going to the cinema?
place	Do you want to come to my place tonight?
up to	What are you up to later?
suggestion	Do you have any suggestions for raising the money?
match	John's first football match is on Saturday.

Module 4: Memories
Page 39 — Birthday memories
ago	Rob's birthday was two months ago.
beach	Shall we go to the beach?
boyfriend	I've got a new boyfriend.
cake	Who wants a piece of cake?
country	Do you prefer living in the country?
early	I was early and had to wait for Debbie.
girlfriend	Has Steve got a girlfriend?
in	They moved here in 1968.
last	Were you out last night?
lunch	We had lunch at a restaurant.
memory	She had very happy memories of her time at college.
picnic	Let's have a picnic on the beach.

Page 40 — School Days
attractive	His new girlfriend is very attractive.
funny	It was one of the funniest films I've ever seen.
old	He was very old when he died.
serious	Philip was a very serious child.
strict	Most of the teachers here are quite strict.
young	Do you enjoy working with young children?

Your letters
angry	I was angry with him for laughing at me.
ask	He wanted to ask his girlfriend something.
class	We are not supposed to talk in class.
head teacher	I was sent to the head teacher.
hey	Hey, that's amazing!
homework	I finished the homework very quickly!
laugh	I can't stop laughing at his jokes.
leave	We had to leave the party at about midnight.
love	I love that dress you're wearing!
pretty	Alison was very pretty.
sense of humour	I really like Sam. He's got a great sense of humour.
show	She showed me a picture of the hotel.
sit	The children all sit on the floor.
student	I don't work. I'm a student.

Page 41 — Excuses
break	It's time for my lunch break.
mobile	Call me on my mobile.
address	My address is 37 King Street, London.
hungry	I'm hungry. What time is lunch?
invite	We invited the Smiths to our house for supper.
present	I went into town to buy a present for my dad.
sandwich	We had chicken sandwiches for lunch.
send	I sent the parcel yesterday.
test	I passed my history test.
cold	I've got a bad cold.
moment	At that moment, the teacher walked in.
next day	I didn't feel very well the next day.
outside	It was a nice sunny day, so we had lunch outside.
stay	I stayed in the car and waited for him.
terrible	I have a terrible headache.
winter	It gets very cold here in winter.
long	She's got long, brown hair.
hair	Her hair is very long.
trip	Dad promised us a trip to Disneyland.
month	I visited the States last month.
demonstration	The photography club arranges demonstrations.

Page 42
partner	John was my partner in the pairwork activity.

Family memories
again	Let's watch that film again.
apple	Can I have an apple, please?
army	My brother joined the army.
die	My grandmother died last year.

WORD LIST

dress	She has a lovely summer dress.
drop	She dropped a glass when she was drying the dishes.
egg	Do you like boiled eggs?
finish	I want to finish this letter before we leave.
granddad	This is my granddad, John.
happily	She laughed happily.
hat	Where's my hat?
love	I really love my mum and dad.
marry	I asked her to marry me.
nervously	"Are you Tim Kelly?" she asked nervously.
parent	I didn't want to disappoint my parents.
problem	There's a problem with the computer.
quickly	Rick ran quickly to the car.
ring	I bought an engagement ring for Mary.
sadly	She smiled sadly.
shopping	Maggie had three bags of shopping.
studies	You need to continue with your studies.
thing	It was a stupid thing to do.
walk over	A man walked over to me in the bar.
war	He was a prisoner during the Vietnam War.
well	I thought the whole team played well.

Page 43

competition	Who won the poetry competition?
orchestra	She plays the violin in the school orchestra.
violin	I learnt to play the violin when I was 5.
about	There were about 40 people at the party.
cafeteria	We ate in a self-service cafeteria.
guy	He's a nice guy.
sit down	She walked over and sat down at my desk.
smile	Sue smiled at the children in a friendly way.
tall	It is one of the tallest trees in the world.
then	Fry the onions. Then add the mushrooms.
walk	We always go for a walk on Sundays.

Adverbs

fast	Stop! I can't run very fast.
happily	They lived happily together for many years.
hard	He works really hard.
nervously	He looked nervously at the angry man.
noisily	He shut the door noisily when he left.
quickly	He speaks very quickly and I can't understand him.
slowly	Ben walks really slowly.
well	Angus speaks French well.

Time linkers

after	Can you help me after your class?
and then	We walked in the park and then went home.
before	Before you go, can you phone Mary?
then	Mary took the bags. Then she left.
when	When I saw him, I gave him the books.

Page 44 — Witnesses

burglar	A burglar stole my watch from my room.
police officer	The police officer arrested him today.
guest	How many guests are coming to your party?
blond	She has short, blond hair.
burglary	He was the victim of a burglary.
get into	How did they get into the house?
happen	Did anything interesting happen at school today?
slim	She was a pretty, slim girl.
sports car	She bought a new sports car.
handbag	There's a pen in my handbag.
post office	Can you take this to the post office, please?

Page 45

concert	We went to a concert last night.
introduce	Eric introduced me to his mother.

Module 5: Fitness

Page 47 — Activities

athletics	We play hockey in winter and do athletics in summer.
basketball	I'm not very good at basketball.
beach volleyball	Beach volleyball is popular in Brazil.
climbing	We go climbing most weekends.
cycling	I go cycling every Sunday.
dancing	We went dancing on New Year's Eve.
exercise	Try to do some exercise every day.
fit	Dancing keeps me fit.
gymnastics	Gymnastics is my favourite sport.
hockey	I played hockey when I was at school.

horse riding	I love watching horse riding.
ice hockey	Ice hockey is more popular in North America than here.
judo	When did judo become an Olympic sport?
rugby	Did you watch the rugby world cup?
skiing	We went skiing in Switzerland.
surfing	We went surfing every day when we were in Australia.
swimming	Do you want to go swimming?
table tennis	I don't like table tennis.
team	I'm in the school football team.
trekking	We like trekking in the summer.
volleyball	We play volleyball at the sports centre.
yoga	Which country does yoga come from?

by	Suzy and I went into town by bus.
cycle	She cycled over to Jane's house.
lift	I took the lift to the tenth floor.
once	She goes out clubbing once a week.
stairs	I ran up the stairs to get my jacket.
take	I'll take the bus home.
time	Your mother called you five times today.
twice	I've been to America twice this year.
popular	He's one of the most popular boys in the school.

Page 48 — Super athletes

amazing	Their apartment is amazing.
artificial	The room was decorated with artificial flowers.
athlete	You can earn a lot of money as a professional athlete.
disabled	There's a lift for disabled people.
fast	He always loved fast cars.
leg	He has artificial legs.
medal	He received a medal for bravery.
project	Cindy's in the library working on her history project.
read	I like reading about space travel.
regular	He returned to his regular duties.
start	What time does the party start?
take part	Hundreds of children took part in the festival.
wear	I decided to wear my blue dress.
win	Mark's team won the basketball tournament.

Page 49

rain	It started to rain just as we were leaving.
song	The kids were singing songs.
drive	Peggy drove to work as usual.
plan	Kathy is already planning her wedding.
prepare	I went home early to prepare for my holiday.
championship	We went to watch the Davis Cup tennis championship.
enjoy	I enjoy cooking when I have time.
exciting	It was a pretty exciting game.
aerobics	She teaches aerobics.
drink	I drink lots of water when I exercise.
festival	The international music festival starts in April.
look after	She looks after her sister's children during the week.
move	The curtain moved in the wind.
rest	Tessa sat on the sofa to rest.
serious	I didn't know if it was a serious offer.

Page 50 — Get fit

advert	Did you see that advert for a Zumba class.
combine	Combine the eggs with a small amount of oil.
customer	We try to keep our customers happy.
difficult	Skiing isn't difficult, but it takes practice.
floor	The toilets are on the top floor.
Latin	I love Latin music.
local	You can get this fruit at your local supermarket.
notice board	The exam results are on the notice board.
only	She got married when she was only 17.
paper	The story was in all the papers.
realistic	The special effects were really realistic.
review	The film got very good reviews.
slow	This computer's very slow!
tower	I live at the top of a tower.
trainer	I need a personal trainer to help me get fit.
useful	I have a useful map of the town centre.
website	For more information about the hotel, visit our website.
lose weight	You lose weight by eating less and exercising more.
marathon	He ran in the New York marathon.
enough	You don't practise your violin enough!
too	It's too hot in here.
garden	The kids are playing in the garden.
square	The park covers two square miles of the city.

Page 51

late	The train was 20 minutes late.
meet	Her mother came to the airport to meet her.
watersports	I enjoy doing different watersports.

Multi-part verbs (2)

come on	Come on, Linda, we're going to be late.
come round	Aunt Flora came round last night.
be into	Ben's really into football.
be up to	It's very quiet. What are the children up to?

Page 52

A fitness freak

lesson	I only had two driving lessons.
session	We have a football training session in the morning.
sporty	I'm not very sporty.
wow	Wow, what a beautiful house!
back	Tracey ran back to the house to get her umbrella.
go away	Go away! Can't you see that I'm busy?
dentist	I need to go to the dentist.
driving	I love driving.
in front	There was a lake in front of the house.

Page 53

Requests and replies

lend	I can lend you £10.
sure	"Is it OK if I sit here?" "Sure."
arrive	The parcel took two weeks to arrive.
borrow	He borrowed £2,000 from his father.
continue	The bad weather will continue for another week.
leave	Oh no! I left my keys in the car!
mine	Could I borrow your pen? I've lost mine.
pair	I need a new pair of trainers.
thirsty	I'm really thirsty. Let's get a drink.
trainer	I need a new pair of trainers.
virtual	I love playing virtual tennis.
work	Does that old radio still work?

Page 54

anyway	It might not rain, but we'll take the umbrella anyway.
cousin	I'm meeting my cousin this afternoon.
invitation	We got an invitation to their New Year's party.
maybe	Maybe the switch is broken.
organise	The school has organised a trip to the sea.
player	He's one of the top tennis players in the school.
accept	Are you going to accept the job?
refuse	I asked Steve to help me, but he refused.
reply	He didn't reply to my question.

Linkers

Because	I didn't play volleyball because I was ill.
So	I was ill so I didn't play volleyball.

Module 6: Age

Page 55

gardening	We did a bit of gardening this afternoon.
probably	I didn't work hard so I'll probably fail my exams.

People

adult	An adult has a lot of responsibilities.
baby	The baby's crying.
child	I lived in the US when I was a child.
pensioner	My grandparents are both pensioners.
teenager	My brother is a teenager.

Personality

clever	She's a very clever student.
hard-working	They are very hard-working pupils.
kind	Grandma is always kind to the children.
moody	After his divorce, he became moody.
outgoing	I want to meet a girl with a very outgoing personality.
shy	Come on, don't be shy.
talkative	My mum is talkative.
tidy	Sarah is very tidy.

Occupations

bus driver	My uncle is a bus driver.
doctor	Nina had to go to the doctor.
engineer	I want to be an engineer.
gardener	Our gardener cuts the grass.
lawyer	I need a lawyer to help me.
nurse	The nurse was very nice to me.
office worker	The office workers are asking for more money.
primary school	My son is still in primary school.
secondary school	I enjoyed my time at secondary school.

shop assistant	The shop assistant was very helpful.
teacher	Miss Lind is my English teacher.
vet	I took my dog to the vet.
waitress	The waitress was very rude.

Page 56

Teenage brains

body	Our bodies need vitamins to stay healthy.
brain	Scientists don't understand how the human brain works.
connection	The brain has many connections.
energy	After I had the flu, I had no energy.
neuron	We studied neurons in biology today.
weigh	My suitcase weighed 20 kilos.
planner	I'm a very good planner.
control	I can't control my emotions.
emotion	The two boys showed no emotion during the trial.

Science today

action	He said he was sorry for his actions.
activity	Criminal activity in the area is increasing.
biological	The company does biological research.
concentrate	Try to concentrate on what you are doing.
consequence	You don't think about the consequences of your actions!
develop	Most plants develop from seeds.
healthy	It's healthy to live near the sea.
less	It cost less than £10.
need	These plants need plenty of light and water.
normal	It's quite normal to feel nervous before you go into hospital.
rhythm	I love the rhythm of the music.
weekend	Did you have a good weekend?
work on	Can I watch you work on your car?

Page 57

meal	We usually have our evening meal at around 7 o'clock.
sofa	Please sit on the sofa.
underground	Shall we go by bus or use the Underground?
revise	I need to revise for my maths test.
article	I read an interesting article about the technology of the future.

Page 58-59

My rights

army	My brother joined the army.
cigarette	Cigarettes are bad for you.
election	Buffy won the election for school president.
leave	Dad leaves work at 6 o'clock every day.
national	I play for the national team.
pay	They always ask for more pay.
smoke	Are you allowed to smoke at work?
vote	The government voted to increase taxes.
campaign	It was a successful election campaign
parliament	Laws are made by parliament.
percent	Thirty percent of people want taxes to be reduced.
representative	Jean Mason is the student representative on the committee.
unfair	It's unfair to make him do all the work.
write	He writes to me every week.

Modifiers

quite	It can be quite cold at night.
really	I really enjoyed our holiday there.
very	Joe looks very happy.
personality	He's not good-looking but he has a great personality.
get up	Lisa got up and made a cup of tea.
stand up	Pete always stands up for his younger brother.
right	All children have the right to free education.

Page 60

Age quiz

ancient	We went to an ancient temple.
go	Her hair went completely white.
grey	He's got grey hair.
memory	She's got a good memory.
age	Jim aged a lot after the accident.
invent	Who invented the first computer?
assistant	My assistant answers the phone and arranges meetings.
examine	The doctor examined me, but could find nothing wrong.

Page 61

Clothes

coat	Put your coat on before you go out.
dress	I love your dress!
jacket	Do I need a jacket?
jeans	He was wearing an old pair of jeans.
jumper	He wore a blue jumper.
shirt	He wore a shirt and tie.
shorts	Jack was wearing a pair of shorts and a T-shirt.

skirt	She wore a white blouse and a blue skirt.
top	I bought a blue top to wear with this skirt.
trousers	I bought a new pair of trousers in the sale.
T-shirt	That's a nice t-shirt.

Describing people in photos

back	The bad kids always sit at the back.
front	I always sit at the front.
left	Walk straight on and you'll see a post office on the left.
middle	The three boys sat on the bench, with Sam in the middle.
next to	Come and sit next to me.
right	Walk straight on and you'll see a post office on the right.

Module 7: Cinema

Page 63 — Types of film

action	I love good action films.
animation	I want to watch an animation.
comedy	All my favourite films are comedies.
documentary	We watched a documentary about dinosaurs.
drama	He wrote a new drama for the BBC.
fantasy	The Lord of the Rings is a fantasy.
film	'Star Wars' is my favourite film.
romantic comedy	My girlfriend likes romantic comedies.
science-fiction	Do you like science-fiction?
thriller	I'm writing a thriller.
western	John Wayne starred in a lot of westerns.

Films

acting	He's brilliant at acting.
actor	He wants to be an actor when he grows up.
actress	Kate Winslet is a famous actress.
brilliant	We had a brilliant time!
dialogue	That film has some great dialogues.
director	Who was the director of 'Star Wars'?
exciting	It was a pretty exciting game.
fantastic	It's a fantastic film!
funny	It was one of the funniest films I've ever seen.
good	Did you have a good holiday?
great	It's really great to be home.
photography	The photography in the film is brilliant.
scene	The battle scenes were very exciting.
special effects	We saw a movie with brilliant special effects.

Page 64 — Film makers

amateur	I'm an amateur photographer.
amazing	Their apartment is amazing.
communicate	The film communicated the feeling of loss.
eccentric	My grandfather was quite eccentric.
film maker	He is a fantastic amateur.
film	No one has ever filmed these animals before.
meeting	Mr Thompson is in a meeting.
original	Her music is very original.
special	We have a very special guest with us this evening.
travel	I made a travel programme for TV.
unicycle	The man in the circus had a unicycle.
video	We watched the video on Youtube.
plan	She plans to get a part-time job.

Page 65

busy	Dad was too busy with work to spend much time with us.
camera	Where did you put my camera?
personal	The story is based on her personal experiences.
critic	The critics praised the play.
nature	I love watching nature programmes on television.
break	I broke my camera yesterday.
flower	There was a vase of yellow flowers by the window.
lose	He lost a lot of money by making bad business decisions.
remember	Remember to buy Anne a card when you go to town.

Page 66 — Film fans

type	I think you should try a different type of exercise.
foreign	The university has a lot of foreign students.
popcorn	We ate popcorn at the cinema.
big name	There were lots of big names at the event.
compare	Look at this list and compare it with yours.
dinner jacket	Men have to wear dinner jackets.
elegant	She wears simple but elegant clothes.
formal	He wasn't comfortable wearing formal clothes.
hospital	My mother is in hospital at the moment.
independent	We went to an independent film festival.
informal	Everyone wore informal clothes.
intention	My original intention was to study in America.
magazine	I bought a magazine to read on the train.

mountain	We spent a weekend climbing in the mountains.
opera house	We went to Sydney Opera House.
practical	We need a practical solution.
prison	He went to prison two years ago.
rainforest	We have to stop the damage to the rainforest.
red carpet	We went to an important red carpet event.
star	She has posters of pop stars on her wall.
station	I'm going to get off at the next station.
tiring	Teaching is a very tiring job.
warm	I want to buy a warm coat to wear this winter.
fan	My brother's a big fan of Madonna.
real	At this price, the tickets are a real bargain.

Page 67 — Adjectives

bored	I'm bored! Can we go home?
exciting	I'm reading a very exciting book.
interested	Sue isn't interested in football.
interesting	She's a very interesting person.
tired	I'm tired so I'm going to bed.
tiring	Playing sport all day is tiring.
relaxed	I feel relaxed after my holiday.
relaxing	A hot bath is relaxing.

Page 68 — Film crews

crew	The film crew work very hard.
decide	Megan decided to go to Denise's party.
equipment	We use the most modern scientific equipment.
exactly	Where exactly did you leave your bike?
instruction	Follow the instructions carefully.
lighting	I control the lighting in the film.
operator	I work as a camera operator.
physical	Do you do much physical exercise?
appearance	He worries about his appearance.
hairdresser	I have an appointment at the hairdresser's.
hairstyle	I like her new hairstyle.
match	Her blue dress matched her eyes.
costume	I wore a terrible costume in the film.

Page 69

romance	The story is a beautiful romance.
agree	Paul and I don't agree on everything.
neither	Neither team played well.
true	"There will be less traffic if we leave early." "That's true."
idea	She has a lot of good ideas.
star	The film stars Drew Barrymore.

Page 70

enter	He decided to enter the poetry competition.
final	On the final day of our holiday, we all went out.
prize	She won first prize in a poetry competition.
closing	Friday is the closing date for the competition.
look forward	I'm looking forward to seeing my family again.
begin	Begin the letter with 'Dear Sir'.
end	I really think we should end this argument.

Module 8: Food and drink

Page 71 — Cereals

bread	She cut another slice of bread.
cereal	I just have cereal for breakfast.
rice	We had chicken with boiled rice.
pasta	I ate pasta the night before the marathon.

Dairy

cheese	Michael wants extra cheese on his pizza.
egg	Do you like boiled eggs?
yoghurt	Mix some yoghurt into the chilli.

Drinks

coffee	Two cups of coffee, please.
milk	Do you want a glass of milk before bed?
tea	I'm going to make a cup of tea.
water	Can I have a glass of water, please?

Fish

salmon	Salmon sandwiches are delicious.
sardine	Sardines are really good for you.
tuna	I have tuna and mayonnaise on my potato.

Fruit

apple	Can I have 5 apples, please?
banana	I bought a bunch of bananas.
cherry	I love cherry yoghurt.

kiwi	Put some kiwi in the fruit salad.
lemon	Can I have a slice of lemon in my drink, please?
melon	Melon is good when it's hot outside.
orange	Taste this sweet, juicy orange.
pear	This pear is very hard.
strawberry	We ate strawberries and cream at Wimbledon.
tomato	I eat tomato on toast when I'm in Spain.

Meat
beef	I don't eat a lot of beef.
chicken	Would you like a chicken sandwich?
lamb	We ate lamb kebabs at the restaurant.
pork	My mum cooked roast pork on Sunday.

Snacks
biscuit	Who wants a chocolate biscuit?
cake	Who wants a piece of cake?
chocolate	Can I have a piece of chocolate?
crisp	I want a bag of crisps.
fruit	Bananas are my favourite fruit.
nuts	Can you eat nuts?
sweet	Don't let the kids eat too many sweets.

Vegetables
beans	Do you want beans?
broccoli	Broccoli is very good for you.
cabbage	They eat a lot of cabbage in Britain.
carrot	Rabbits eat carrots all day.
cucumber	Let's have a cucumber and tomato salad.
lettuce	Do you want lettuce in your sandwich?
mushroom	Can I have a pizza with pepperoni and mushrooms, please.
onion	I'm growing onions in the garden.
potato	You make chips from potatoes.

Page 72 — Eating in the future
around	I went to the house, but there was no one around.
chip	Would you like chips with your burger?
culture	Food is an important part of our culture.
disappear	The rainforests are disappearing quickly.
dish	The restaurant offers a lot of French dishes.
fast food	We can get some fast food when we go out.
fresh	Eat lots of fresh fruit and vegetables.
future	In the future, almost everyone will have a computer.
habit	Changing your eating habits can be really difficult.
little	There's very little work to do.
mineral	Minerals are important for good health.
quick	We need a quick decision on this.
salad	Meals are served with chips and salad.
sandwich	We had chicken sandwiches for lunch.
sushi	Sushi is my favourite Japanese dish!
vegetarian	I don't eat chicken. I'm a vegetarian.
vitamin	Oranges contain a lot of vitamin C.

Page 73
become	Dad started to become angry.
unhealthy	I don't eat unhealthy food like burgers and chips.
ethnic	We met people from different ethnic groups.
overweight	He's an overweight businessman.
chef	He's a fantastic chef.
adventure	It's a book about Johnson's adventures at sea.
fall in love	My parents fell in love when they were 16.
scientist	Scientists found a cure for the disease.

Page 74-75 — Good food
continent	Africa is a continent that contains lot of different countries.

Food from the sky
bee	I keep bees in my garden.
carbon dioxide	Trees change carbon dioxide into air.
chemical	Some of these chemicals are very dangerous.
climate	The climate in the Maldives is hot and sunny.
create	The new rules will create a lot of problems.
factory	She works in a chocolate factory.
female	I can hear a female voice; it's the girl who lives next door.
gas	Carbon monoxide is a dangerous gas.
grow	We grow our own vegetables.
hen	The eggs are from my hens.
honey	I like honey on my bread.
insect	I study insects.
omelette	Do you like cheese omelettes?
organic	I make everything with organic vegetables.
owner	Who is the owner of the company?
the planet	Is the climate of our planet really changing?
roof	The roof of the church had been damaged in a storm.

supermarket	I have to go to the supermarket after work.
sweet	This chocolate sauce is very sweet.
synthetic	The material in my jumper is synthetic.
urban	I work on an urban development.
visit	We're hoping to visit Rome while we're in Italy.
webcam	You can watch the birds in their nest on a webcam.
flat	I need a flat surface to work on.

Page 76 — Nutrition
cookbook	He bought me a lovely cookbook for my birthday.
hungry	I'm hungry. What time is lunch?
nutrition	Nutrition is important for an athlete.
regularly	Delete your old emails regularly.
tip	Can you give me any tips on how to lose weight?

Module 9: Countries
Page 79 — Countries
population	What's the population of Tokyo?
centre	Find the centre of the circle using your ruler.
east	The sun rises in the east.
north	I think we should walk north.
south	Where is south?
west	The sun sets in the west.
beach	Shall we go to the beach?
forest	He got lost in the forest.
lake	I have a boat on the lake.
lovely	She has a lovely face.
mountain	We spent a weekend climbing in the mountains.
national park	We went to a few national parks in the USA.

Seasons
autumn	This shrub has orange berries in autumn.
spring	In spring all the plants start to grow again.
summer	Last summer we went on vacation to Florida.
winter	It gets very cold here in winter.

Weather
cloudy	It's very cloudy today.
cold	Hurry up! I'm getting cold.
dry	It was a very dry summer.
foggy	It was so foggy we couldn't see the other side of the road.
hot	It was a very hot day.
icy	It's an icy winter morning.
rainy	What a rainy day!
snowy	I was very snowy yesterday.
sunny	Let's go to the beach. It's sunny.
windy	It was too windy to go for a walk.

Page 80 — Abroad
actually	"I don't really want to go out. Actually, I'd like to go home."
around	People around the world admire his singing.
beginning	In the beginning, the company was very successful.
essay	I had to write an essay on Shakespeare.
feel	I felt cold and lonely.
horrible	That dress is horrible.
joke	I heard a funny joke the other day.
maths	I study maths at university.
opinion	George has strong opinions about divorce.
philosophy	I'm interested in Eastern philosophy
politics	She wanted a career in politics.
serious	Luckily there were no serious problems.
subject	My favourite subject is English.
topic	The main topic of conversation was the party.
specific	The books are designed for this specific age group.
unique	Every person's fingerprints are unique.

Page 81 — Asking about places
disco	Are you going to the school disco?
bookshop	I need to get some books from the bookshop.
library	Did you study in the library yesterday?
gym	I go to the gym twice a week.
lab	I work in a computer lab.
drama	Miss Jay is our drama teacher.
spend	Brendan spent over £600 on his new mountain bike.
understand	I couldn't understand what the men were saying.

Page 82-83 — Costa Rica
central	We travelled through Central America last year.
amazing	Their apartment is amazing.
Caribbean	We went on a boat across the Caribbean sea.
crocodile	I am scared of crocodiles.
eco-tourism	I have an eco-tourism business.

elephant	Elephants live for a very long time.
feature	This new software has some very useful features.
giraffe	Giraffes live in Africa.
green	We should develop greener forms of transport.
hiking	We went hiking in the mountains.
lion	The male lion has long thick hair around his neck.
monkey	There were monkeys in the trees.
Pacific	We swam in the Pacific.
rent	We rent the flat from my uncle.
river	We swam in the river.
sloth	Look at the sloth sleeping in the tree.
tourist	I showed a group of Japanese tourists around the city.
turtle	I had a turtle when I was young.
volcano	I walked up a volcano in South America.
white-water rafting	I went white-water rafting in South America.
tourism	The island's main industry is tourism.
activity	Criminal activity in the area is increasing.
weather	Did you have good weather on your trip?

Page 84 European tour
group	A fight started between two groups of men.
guide	The guide pointed out the cathedral on the left.
lost	It was such a big building that I got lost in it!
mention	I'll mention it to Rob.
menu	The waiter brought us the menu to look at.
say	What did you say?
sign	We followed the signs for Birmingham.
strange	I could hear strange noises.
useful	We need a useful map of the town centre.
passport	I lost my passport.
anniversary	Today is my parents' 25th wedding anniversary.
lucky	He's lucky to have such a good job.
smile	Sue smiled at the children in a friendly way.
bar	I just met a really old friend in the hotel bar.
go out	She started going out with him when she was 16.
explore	They spent the afternoon exploring the town.

Page 85
arrange	I arranged a football practice for tomorrow.
parrot	The parrot talks to me.
route	This is the shortest route to school.
cross	Thousands of refugees crossed the border.
along	We were walking along the road, talking.
past	He watched the cars go past.
in front	The car in front stopped suddenly.
turn	Turn right at Baldwin Street, and then turn left.
building	The science laboratory is in this building.

Page 86
show	She is in a show on Broadway.
tango	We watched tango on the streets of Buenos Aires.
description	Carson gave the police a description of the car.

Module 10: Gadgets
Page 87 Computers
desktop	I do most of my work on my desktop computer.
laptop	I use my laptop on the train.
net book	I carry my net book with me everywhere.
tablet	I don't have a tablet.

Gadgets
digital camera	This new digital camera is amazing.
DVD player	We need to buy a new DVD player.
Sat Nav	The Audi A6 comes with Sat-Nav and climate control.
phone	I can check my emails on my smart phone.
USB flash drive	My documents are all on my USB flash drive.
video camera	Can I borrow your video camera?
video game console	He plays on his video games console too much.

Online
check email	I need to check my emails.
download	You can download music and videos from the Internet.
go online	For more information, please go online.
message	Send me a message later.
play	He plays computer games all day.
program	It's a fantastic computer program.
send	I sent him a message about the meeting.
upload	I uploaded a video onto YouTube.

Page 88 Gadget zone
directions	A woman gave us directions to the theatre.
bath	Sally's in the bath.
comment	My teacher made some very useful comments.
creative	He's a very creative artist.
hammock	We slept in hammocks on the beach.
influence	Kate used her influence to get her friend a job.
map	I collect old maps.
pocket	He took some money out of the pocket of his jeans.
problem	She's had a lot of personal problems recently.
sandal	Do you have a pair of leather sandals?
screen	I'm looking for a television with a 26-inch screen.
unnecessary	Testing cosmetics on animals is unnecessary.
wrong	That's the wrong answer.

Page 89
old	I liked my old school better than this one.
surf	I surfed the web all day.

Page 90 Technology
connection	They're offering free Internet connection.
expert	Bomb experts made the device safe.
late	It's late and I'm tired.
nervous	Julie looked nervous before the test.
nowadays	More people work at home nowadays.
psychologist	I'm studying to be a psychologist.
tunnel	Trains go through the Channel Tunnel.
use	The new drug has many uses.

Page 91
laboratory	We worked hard in the laboratory.
secretary	Call my secretary to arrange a meeting.

Page 92 Pet Gadgets
design	The company is designing a golf course.
inventor	The inventor of the telephone is Alexander Graham Bell.
life jacket	You have to wear a life jacket on the boat.
sunglasses	She was wearing sunglasses.
test	The school is testing some new educational software.
abroad	I spent six months travelling abroad.

Page 93
battery	I need to recharge the batteries for my camera.
design	I like the design of this room.
GPS	I bought a GPS watch for when I go running.
life	These batteries have a very short life.
long	These batteries are long-life.
memory	How much memory does your computer have?
navigation	The navigation of this website is great.
system	We're having a new computer system installed.
touch screen	The touch screen works well.
unhappy	Barbara had a very unhappy childhood.